WORKING WATERCRAFT

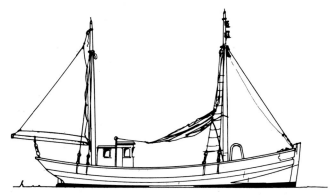

WORKING WATERCRAFT

a Survey of the Surviving Local
Boats of Europe and America

Thomas C. Gillmer

Patrick Stephens Limited **PSL**

LONDON

ISBN 0 85059 126 0

Published in Great Britain by Patrick Stephens Limited,
9 Ely Place, London ECIN 6SQ
First published in the United States
by International Marine Publishing Company
Camden, Maine 04843

*Printed in the United States of America
Designed by Melbourne Smith*

CONTENTS

INTRODUCTION

I N THE WORLD of ships and boats there is an ever-diminishing number of small watercraft that have always managed to remain relatively obscure. They are the boats that are indigenous to their regions of origin, primarily devised and worked by their owners. Often poor, the owners of these boats seem to be as timeless as their boats. Indeed, these boats are a foggy mirror reflecting the past, since they seldom benefit from the skill and progressive outlook of professional designers. Their unprogressive and conservative origins are, therefore, the measure of their significance. Their structure and configurations arise from memory and generations of experience and often superstitions, all tightly bound by tradition. Yet there is a quality in these workboats that transcends tradition. It is hoped that this study, with its descriptions and analyses of today's working boats, will reveal some of the beauty and functional design of these boats.

First, some basic limitations to this study must be mentioned. I have, in a way, described "indigenous boats." I hasten to add that there are often factors that confuse the indigenous character of a boat. There are, of course, the obvious elements that mark a craft as *not* being indigenous. Boats of professional design, factory-built and sold in export markets, are certainly not indigenous. Large fishing craft of sophisticated technological design have in recent years assumed cosmopolitan qualities. They have become so efficient with their modern gear and so capable with their professionally designed hulls that they range thousands of miles over the world's oceans. I have confined my observations to boats that still exist today — boats still built with little access to the modern world's economy and technology and that are of so limited a size that they cannot or will not cruise very far from their native ports. This size cannot be precisely stated, but for the purpose here, never exceeds 100 feet in over-all length or 90 tons displacement, and even these dimensions are exceptional.

The purpose of this study, then, is mainly to reveal the nature of small watercraft presently at work in the regions of their origin, built and owned by craftsmen and sailors so long unknown and forgotten by society. It is not possible to view and describe all such existing boats nor would it seem wise to try. Consequently, the examples for description and illustration are the result of a considered and representative selection. They are selections from the uncounted number of working boats of North American and European waters.

It should be emphasized that this is a transient survey. While I do not think that indigenous working boats will entirely disappear from the coasts and harbors of the world, there is, on the other hand, substantial evidence that many have gone and are going. It is, of course, an ever-changing scenario.

In the following chapters it is obvious that, while some types of craft have become obsolete, there are others, too, that are of recent origin. It does not appear, however, that there is a balance of replacement of older types by newer ones. This could be the result of an ecological imbalance. As pollution increases, and the number of fish declines, the number of working boats will also diminish. These changes are now well advanced, and the effects of pollution are alarmingly apparent in many American waters, in the North Sea, and in nearly all of the Mediterranean.

The necessity of a survey of the current tenuous existence of small indigenous working boats is obvious. The boats that are described or observed on the following pages are still alive, some barely so, but this is a contemporary comment — a picture of the boats at this point in time. If the reader, therefore, does not find any or many of his favorite, most admirable, beautiful, and capable working boats on these pages, it is most likely because they no longer exist. This is not intended to be a history or an encyclopedia. Other accounts of small indigenous watercraft have been published, and most of these valuable works are historical in approach. Yet there are segments here, too, of the history of boat construction and development, but only in the context of the origins of the still-functioning working boats that are indigenous to their own regions.

The fast-diminishing working sailboats deserve extra mention here. There seems to be no geographic or political explanation for the continued use of working sailboats, and certainly there is no technological justification for it. Though economics appear to be the primary determining factor, sailing workboats may be found in regions of the world that are either rich and populated or remote and barren. There is no pattern or logical explanation for their continuity in the modern world.

Most commercial sailing ships disappeared or were replaced by mechanically powered vessels in the last part of the nineteenth and the early part of the twentieth centuries. Yet today there are, in nearly every western sea, areas where slower-moving maritime commerce finds a place for boats with mast and sail. Those that remain are disappearing quickly, however.

Because fishing is no longer a small business, the sailing workboats engaged in fishing will be the first to go of those that remain. A few years ago, I observed a large Brixham trawler working its way under sail into the North Sea. Yet to what purpose? To work in competition with the new and efficient trawlers and drifters pushed by heavy, reliable diesels and equipped with modern, powered fishing gear? The smallest and the poorest boats engaged in marginal economies — the traders among remote islands and ports — will prevail longer and most likely will be helped along by sail. Many such trading sailboats ply among the Baltic, Bahama, and Aegean islands. For instance, Galway hookers still carry turf fuel to the Aran islanders.

The future of the legally protected fishing craft under sail is clouded and problematical. But even with legal protection, the continued existence of working sailboats is contingent on economics and human attitudes. They can exist in areas where a healthy and vigorous demand exists for special sea-food products, such as oysters and prawns, and in areas where these products can be harvested more efficiently by sail than by power. Oysters are apparently not so appealing to Americans as they are to the British, and the prices do not hold as firmly here. The sailing work boats of the Chesapeake may have been retained beyond their time. It is not as easy to interest or stimulate young fishermen or to encourage new owners to invest in replacement craft. The powered patent-tongers can make as much or more on a lesser catch because their overhead and maintenance is not as much as a skipjack's. If the laws, which are basically conservation measures, continue, although in recent years they have been relaxed, the demise of the skipjacks will only be delayed a little longer. There is a continuing decline in number. In 1967 there were 60 licensed skipjacks working, in 1968 there were 52, and now there are but 40 or so.

An impressive number of American sailboat types, reflecting the various requirements and imaginative building skills of Yankee seamen and builders, have passed into history. The great Gloucester and Nova Scotia schooners, Friendship sloops, Tancook whalers, older Block Island schooners, pinkies, crabbing sharpies, Hatteras sloops, Gulf schooners, and San Francisco fellucas are being joined by the Chesapeake bugeyes as a part of American maritime history. All of these craft are well documented. They will not be soon forgotten.

On the other side of the Atlantic the attrition of sailing craft types has been continuing for a longer time and involves a greater number of types. At this time, the Europeans cannot show many more indigenous types of sailing boats than can the Americans.

Obviously, the future of working sailboats is mixed. Those that remain seem to be under a conditional verdict of death, with only the shred of a possibility of commutation to life at hard labor in the most impoverished environments. But for some, the future might not be a dead-end road. Absolute predictions are impossible. Our great-grandchildren may yet enjoy the sight of a stray lateen-rigged coaster working its way out of a tiny forgotten port in Tuscany, the Bahamas, or Portugal. The sailboats that remain most likely will be sailed by sailors or fishermen who have found a local market sufficient for their fish or cargo. These boatmen will always be impoverished but independent souls who value personal freedom and the wind that moves their boats. Their return in pay is uncertain, and their work is rugged and thankless; they must accept these things. The future of sail depends on these men already.

My very strong feeling that the destiny of the boat is involved with the destiny of men should be apparent throughout the following discussions. Any man who reflects for a moment on the nature of a boat must agree with such a fundamental premise. Man, from the beginning, could never have freed himself from his terrible, primordial isolation without the aid of water transport. It was watercraft that carried him out on the world's first wet natural roads to begin his long, slow, inevitable journey toward civilization; with boats he communicated and carried his goods of trade and habitation. With ships, he still does, but in the workboat of today, the small indigenous ones, we can still find some primeval elements and see the marks of hand tools and human skills like those used at first. So we have tried to reflect on and to record some of these things.

Annapolis, Maryland

ACKNOWLEDGEMENTS

The preparation and writing of this survey of present-day indigenous western boats was a most pleasant occupation. I do not really remember when it began and it is difficult to say when it ended. Along the way, there were many people and friends whose interest and help were greatly used and appreciated. For example, there is my friend Nicolas Kenyeres, a boatbuilder in Barcelona, Spain, who lent his valuable time to indulge my interest in Catalonian boats by transporting me up the coast to the Costa Brava. He stopped at every little cove and fishing harbor to inspect the boats with me and interpret the fishermen's remarks. There are international experts, such as Dr. Henning Henningsen at the fine museum of Elsinor, Denmark, who has allowed the use of his line drawings of indigenous Danish craft. There was Elmer Collemer of Camden, Maine, a master boatbuilder who acquainted me with the better features of lobster boats nearly twenty years ago. And long before that, when I was what is now called a teenager, there was my old friend and sailor George Woodside, from Prince Edward Island. He built my first boat and it was a lovely, clinker-built sailing skiff of fourteen feet, which he built by eye and instinct. There were others, many of whom helped me over the years past. I originally wanted to supply all the illustrations myself, and with the sketches and drawings, except as noted above, I have. Perhaps less than half of the photographs are mine, but there are many others which are more rare and of a quality which I could not match. These are credited individually in the back of the book. To all of these individuals who lent me photographs, many of whom are close friends and share my interest in and fascination with boats, I wish to extend my sincere thanks for their help.

In addition to these friends, I am much beholden to a number of cooperative institutions who have made their photograph collections available. These are:

Field Museum of Natural History, Chicago
Norwegian Boat Export Board, Oslo
Science Museum, London
Universitetets Oldsaksamling, Oslo
National Fisherman, Camden
Bibliotheque et Musee, Marseilles

Finally, The Peabody Museum of Salem and the *American Neptune* editors are especially to be thanked for their permission to use the sketches from Antoine Roux's original sketch books as well as the pen and ink sketches by myself which were originally published in 1941 in Vol. I, No. 4, and Vol. II, No. 1, of the *American Neptune* in the article "Present-Day Craft and Rigs of the Mediterranean" by Lieut. (jg) T. C. Gillmer, U. S. Navy.

WORKING WATERCRAFT

1 / SHAPE, STRUCTURE, AND STYLE

THE BOAT is man's own invention. Arrived at through a driving need for mobility, it is surely the most important of his contrivances. It has from the beginning enabled the species to move forth, to rid itself of the repressiveness of its insular, clannish communities, to sow the seeds and plant the knowledge on farther fields, in a word, to grow, and expand, to create trade, effect communication, ultimately to generate the basis for civilization. This vehicle of transport on the only roads of a primitive world began with the smallest and crudest of structures.

The first of such structures that could be truly called a boat has not survived for us to see. However, with a little reflection aided by the knowledge of the craft of contemporary primitive tribes, archeological studies, and the primitive boats still found in the midst of the most advanced communities, we are able to make some reasonable estimates of their origin.

Confronted with the problem of transport and personal conveyance on the water, primitive man turned to several tentative solutions. The trunk of a fallen tree could be, and no doubt was, the basis of one most successful solution. Woven reeds, forming primitive baskets and containers when plastered with resin, mud, or other more suitable fill, provided more portable watercraft. These probably gave way to the more practical and durable frame-skin craft. Indeed, these three types of primitive boats exist today: the dug-out log, the woven reed boat, and the frame-skin craft. They exist in many parts of the world in an assortment of individual configurations, some most crude, and others of remarkable refinement. Many are most useful and capable of extremely good performance.

In every growing culture in the long human story, the first step toward solving the problem of water transport began with one or more of the three boat types outlined above. As the growing cultures developed greater knowledge (often with the help of the primitive boat) and acquired better tools, the watercraft naturally developed too. The first propulsive device was the paddle, followed by the oar, then the crude, single square sail, and then a fore and aft sail. Propulsion was improved by multiple sails and ingenious rigs. Larger, framed, planked hulls with keels were developed. Steering oars gave way to rudders, and boats finally became ships. But the basic, common boat never disappeared; there was always the boat for the poorer, individual small-businessman of the sea.

In the course of man's being, several human cultures have frequently existed, advancing independently, and at differing stages of growth. It is thus possible, in a crude way and only up to an obscure limit, to measure a society's development by examining the state of refinement of its watercraft. The Norse people, for example, who were later to become the finest of seafarers, were using frame-skin boats when the Greeks were roving the Mediterranean in great triremes and were trading in their merchant ships with much of civilization.

Later, as evidenced by the remains of a boat found in Bjorke, Sweden, and dated at 100 A.D., Norse boat construction rapidly improved. The boat was planked in wood but the bottom was a hollowed log. It was 24 feet long and propelled by paddles. In a peat bog in Schleswig called Nydam, a boat was found in 1863 that was also obviously Scandinavian and dated at about 300 A.D. This boat was planked in a more sophisticated way, clinker-built and fully framed with oak. It was 75 feet long, 11 feet wide, and fitted for 30 oars. The Norse culture was now rapidly overtaking that of the languishing Mediterraneans, but Norse builders needed to discover yet the techniques of handling sail, and the value and a local source of hand-wrought iron. The Nydam boat shows in her construction an embryonic keel, which is merely a heavier bottom center plank with a heavy exterior channel. But on a later boat found at Kvalsund, Norway, in 1920, dated at about 600 A.D., there is a distinct external, vertical keel. This boat is about 60 feet long and 10½ feet wide. It has the deeper, rounded sections with upswept ends of a boat for offshore use. Strangely, no mast was yet in evidence, but then it was still only 600 A.D., and the Norwegians were not yet inspired to travel far beyond their fjord-pierced coast where there was always good shelter and a friendly anchorage, and the wind was light, variable and unreliable.

But again, a boat of only two centuries later was found in Oseberg, Norway, south of Oslo. It is a formidable and beautiful example of architectural achievement. While much of Europe lay dormant in the shroud of feudalism the Scandinavians advanced the technology of boatbuilding as far as, or farther than any culture. Their boats were, from this Oseberg example, superbly structured with the best materials for the building of wooden boats in any age. While the Norse boats were open, their hull configurations and sophisticated structures by the end of the first millennium A.D. compare favorably with any wood boat that could be built today for the functional activity for which they were designed.

The Oseberg boat, shown in Figure 1-1, while a superb example of boatbuilding, was not itself intended for use as either a seagoing warcraft or a trading vessel. The elaborate decorative treatment of the craft together with the burial treasure it contained indicate that it was the ceremonial pleasure boat or royal yacht of the queen who has been identified with the remains. Such a boat was called a *karv*. A more rugged and plainer Viking boat of the same period or a little later has been found nearby on a farm named Gokstad. This boat, which measures 76½ feet in length and 17 feet in beam, was well able to cruise offshore and move safely in a seaway. With greater freeboard and more heavily framed with sixteen lapped and riveted oak planks per side, the Gokstad "ship" represents the best example of the early Norse seacraft (see Figure 1-3).

Both the Oseberg and Gokstad boats show the same building techniques. One such basic technique is that used to join the frames and planking, a method so sound that it should still be practiced. The early Scandinavian builders seem to have been acquainted with the need for an independent

1-1   The Oseberg ship was restored after it was recovered from a Viking burial mound. Buried around 900 A.D., this ship is a superb example of shipbuilding skill.

1-1

1-2　This small Norse craft was also found in the Gokstad grave. It is a better example of the more simple boats used by the people, the fishermen, and the itinerant trader. This boat is less than 30 feet long, and her construction is the same as today's small open boats and skiffs of western Norway.

1-3　The Gokstad ship, a Viking vessel for sea voyages and conquest. Such boats as this were used by the Norsemen who fought in England, Ireland, Iceland, and elsewhere. The Norse colonists followed later in smaller, beamier, and more humble boats.

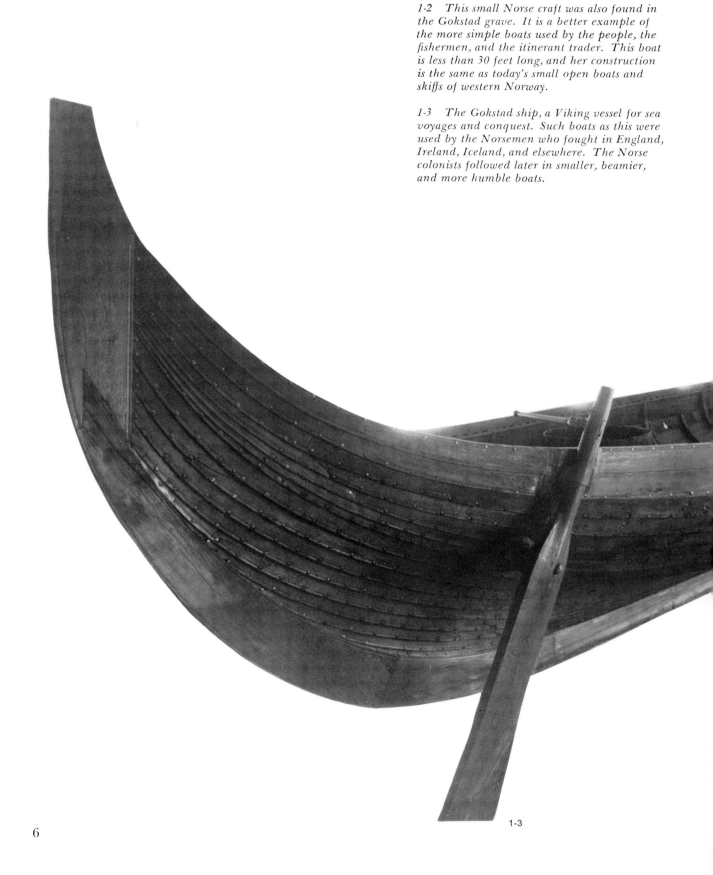

1-3

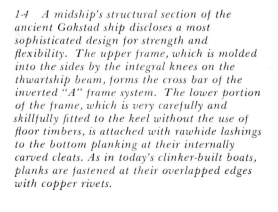

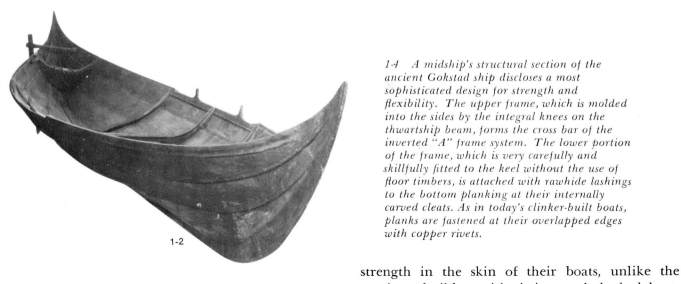

1-4 *A midship's structural section of the ancient Gokstad ship discloses a most sophisticated design for strength and flexibility. The upper frame, which is molded into the sides by the integral knees on the thwartship beam, forms the cross bar of the inverted "A" frame system. The lower portion of the frame, which is very carefully and skillfully fitted to the keel without the use of floor timbers, is attached with rawhide lashings to the bottom planking at their internally carved cleats. As in today's clinker-built boats, planks are fastened at their overlapped edges with copper rivets.*

1-2

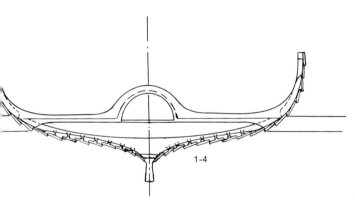

1-4

strength in the skin of their boats, unlike the southern builders with their carvel-planked boats where the planking was fastened in separate strakes to a massive frame. The boats of these Vikings have strong, natural-grown frames, but throughout their curvature they are separated from the planking by projecting, integral cleats on the inner surface of the planks which are lashed to the frames by rawhide thongs in a secure but flexible system. The overlapping edges of the planking are through-riveted in the same manner that present day clinker-built boats are fastened with rivets at close intervals. Such construction provides a relatively light hull with great longitudinal strength in the skin, which is firmly held in shape by a complete inner frame. Thus with a continuous, single-piece external keel scarfed to the stem and stern posts, the hull structure of the Norse boats provided the strongest of craft with a strength-to-weight ratio that can seldom be exceeded today with any material or building technique.

The old Norse rowing boat or skiff structure, evident in the several small boats discovered with the Gokstad ship, is remarkably similar to the present Norwegian skiffs. This is further discussed in Chapter 3. Figure 1-2 shows one of these graceful little boats, which has three lapped planks on each side, cant frames of natural crooks in the ends, and three intermediate frames. The center frame forms a shallow inverted "A". This planking and framing system is identical to that of the skiffs still built in Norway (and nowhere else).

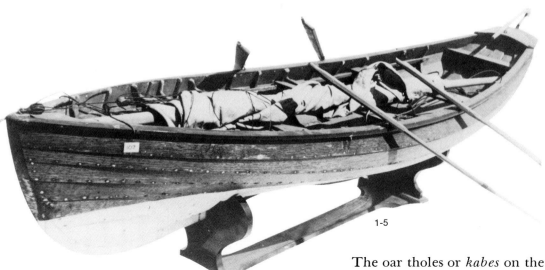

1-5

1-5 *A model of a Yorkshire coble, a boat built by the methods used and introduced by the Norsemen more than 12 centuries ago. The vast majority of the smaller beach craft of the British Isles and northern Europe are still of this same clinker (lapstrake) construction invented by the early Norsemen.*

1-6 *This middle structural section reveals the methods and thinking of Egyptian boatbuilders of three and one half millenniums ago. This midsection of Pharaoh Cheops' boat of 2680 B.C. is not based on speculation. The actual boat is intact today, having been removed from a sealed tomb near the Great Pyramid of Cheops in 1955. It is slowly and carefully being restored to its original shape.*

The oar tholes or *kabes* on the rail are of the same single crook pattern also used today, but are more nicely carved and finished. Curiously, these small, ancient skiffs are fitted with proper little steering oars with tillers on the starboard side like their larger sisters.

These Norse relics, when compared with other craft, give us a very true and clear picture of the development of modern boat structures in northern Europe and much of northeastern United States and Canada. The lapstrake hull, with its light but strong system of framing, can be found in boatbuilding throughout the entire Anglo-Saxon culture. Lapstrake or "clinker-built" boats (as they came to be called) are found on the beaches and in the harbors of New England, Nova Scotia, Ireland, Scotland, England, and most of the northern European countries. Such construction allows a natural boat to form by laying one plank over the edge of the adjacent lower one. This makes a double thickness at the plank edges that is the equivalent of a longitudinal stringer, which results in a total structure of longitudinals that needs only light, steam-bent frames to reinforce the internal form. In boats of such a nature, deck beams or continuous decks are often not necessary for added rigidity.

This ingenious system has some minor drawbacks. The exterior of the hull is one of longitudinal ridges and crevices that produce unnecessary hydrodynamic drag. Such boats, unless expertly built, tend to be a bit leaky and are difficult to caulk. Finally, in a clinker-built boat it is very difficult to cover up bad workmanship.

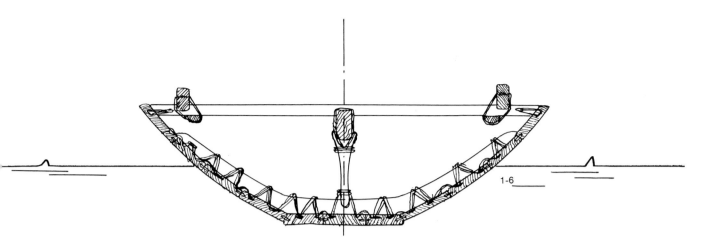

1-6

Compared to other methods, lapstrake construction is a relatively new boatbuilding approach. The far older method, which in the dim reaches of early civilizations improved on the primitive dugout log, is the smooth-planked carvel hull. This method, as far as can be ascertained, was first used by the early Egyptians.

Sparse archeological finds indicate that boats were becoming more refined sometime in the first or second dynasty before the Old Kingdom, approximately between 3000 and 2700 B.C. They were obviously more than shaped bundles of papyrus reeds or built-up log canoe-type craft. At this time, men had acquired considerable skill in the use of metal tools. The Bronze Age was yet to come, but in Egyptian tombs of this time have been found such tools as adzes, chisels, awls, and saw blades, all of pure hardened copper. Cedar wood was imported from Lebanon, rope was made of flax and long, fibrous halfa grass, and sails were (on the better boats) of linen. There is no reason why boats could not have been made of wood planks at this time. But for boats of this period and before, there are no clear examples — either drawings, models, or relics — that give many clues about their structures or configurations.

Egyptologists have recently discovered a completely preserved boat that was built a little later, but still 4,600 years ago. This craft, which has been identified as the Boat of Cheops, was taken from a boat grave near the great Pyramid of Cheops in 1955, but until the present time there has been no information available on its construc-

tion and condition of restoration. Admirers of boats are indebted to Mr. Bjorn Landstrom, the Swedish boat historian and artist, for his superb description and illustrations of this ancient and beautifully built vessel in *Ships of the Pharaohs.*

The Boat of Cheops can fairly well serve as the original model for the emerging techniques that were to lead to the well-known methods of wood boatbuilding used almost universally. This original boat lacks only a few of the basic ingredients. The cross section shown in Figure 1-6 is the elemental structural section. The boat has no keel of course, but has three broad, heavy bottom planks. Rising from this flat bottom with considerable flare on each side, nearly like the sides of a giant dory, are four side planks fastened edge to edge. The deck structure is supported by heavy, flat deck beams, closely spaced, which are let into holes in the upper or sheer plank. On the centerline directly under the deck beams is the Egyptian substitute for the keel. It is a long, continuous wood girder set on edge and notched to allow the deck beams to cross over flush, and provides longitudinal support. This girder ends just short of the bow and stern, and is about the length of the waterline. It is supported at regular intervals by column-like stanchions resting on transverse foundation members. This type of transverse member might be called a frame, but it does not, in my opinion, serve the same function as the conventional transverse boat frame. The Egyptian builders had something else in mind when they fitted this stretcher-foundation to the bottom and part way up the side. It is a

1-7 This is another existing boat of Ancient Egypt, dated about 2000 B.C. This boat was discovered in a boat grave with several others near Sesostris's Pyramid in 1893. Notice the notched sheer plank which allows the deck beams to protrude, an Egyptian practice that later persisted for over 2,000 years of European boatbuilding.

1-8 This midsection of the Sesostris boat shows the absence of structural frames and keel. Such a boat, with heavy, hewn planks edge-fastened with tenons and keys, is structurally adequate without frames if the length is not great. This boat is about 31 feet long and 8 feet in beam. Its construction, as that of the Cheops boat, is the very root and origin of today's carvel planking system.

supporting base more akin to that member in modern boats called a floor. It actually, and I believe with intention, makes a complete, longitudinal centerline truss. The Egyptians' knowledge and understanding of engineering were the most advanced of any civilization's for 2,000 years, until the Romans borrowed and built from it.

The basic Egyptian methodology in boat construction was to use heavy, thick planking, keyed or morticed together. With heavier bottom strakes, the whole form was strengthened and held in shape by a truss system, either external, internal or both. This complex truss system, as is evident in the reassembled Cheops boat, was absolutely necessary in the absence of the keel and transverse (or longitudinal) framing. (This boat is 138 feet long, almost 19 feet in beam, and about 12 feet in depth of hold. It would displace about 40 tons.)

In smaller Egyptian craft (30 to 32 feet in length), of which three examples from a later dynasty exist today, there are no frames nor is there any truss system for longitudinal support. (See Figure 1-7.) The planking is joined together by "butterfly"-type keys (still used in wood joinery by oriental craftsmen). The planking is thick and so·well joined by scarfs and keys that, together with deck beams, it holds the hull's shape with reasonable integrity. (See Figure 1-8.)

It is safe to say, in light of the Cheops discovery and others, that the Egyptians did *not* use transverse frames or keels until the second millennium, B.C. They were able, however, to build long, planked boats that held their shape with considerable strength, at least for a time. However, the Egyptian boats needed keels and frames for serious voyages in the Mediterranean Sea, the Red Sea, or Indian Ocean — the real seas. Their truss construction was good engineering theory, but the fastenings were not dependable. The fastenings were bindings of rope fiber or heavy twine laced through holes in the adjacent wood members. With stress and moisture, such connections become tired and move and loosen. Boats such as these long, arched Egyptian river craft surely must have been short lived when they ventured out on the Mediterranean.

Evidence of further attempts to control the slack in Egyptian boats of a few hundred years after the Cheops boat is apparent. For example, a different truss system was used in the seagoing ships of King Sahure in 2500 B.C. Reliefs on this king's tomb clearly show a row of vertical centerline stanchions supporting a long hawser-bridge attached at each end of the boat to a girdle round the bow and at the stern. The stanchions provided a much deeper web and undoubtedly rested on the frame-like floors in the bottom. The hawser-bridge truss above the deck was equipped with a tourniquet rod thrust through the strands of the twisted hawser for periodic tension applications. This anti-hogging truss arrangement was to continue in Egyptian vessels for at least ten dynasties, while the internal heavy deck girder under the deck beams also continued in use. It was not until well into the eighteenth dynasty (about 1500 B.C.) that any evidence of a keel was to be seen in Egyptian boats.

1-7

The use of a keel — a remarkable and fundamental milestone in the construction of boats — was probably not an Egyptian development. The Kingdom of Ancient Egypt had prospered and dominated all other civilizations for well over 2,000 years, but her boats were, at the end of the Middle Kingdom (1800 B.C.) not only becoming stagnant in design but suffering some retrogression. The sea was no longer an unchallenged extension of the Pharaoh's empire. Newer and more agressive sea peoples living among the Aegean islands began in the early second millennium B.C. to roam the entire eastern Mediterranean and probe deeply into the western Mediterranean and doubtless beyond. While there is only the sketchiest evidence of the structure of boats of the Minoans, their extensive sea trade and the home environment of their islands suggests that the boats they used must have been lighter and inherently stronger in structure than those of the Egyptians. There is but one way to build stronger and lighter boats than the Egyptian type. That way is to use planking of lesser thickness over a strong transverse frame erected on a continuous keel-stem backbone.

In restrospect, the early Egyptian boats were a most progressive step forward into a fundamental technology. The Egyptians were the first to build up a wood shell of planks into a true and often magnificent boat. Though the direction they took was the most logical to get away from the dugout log, these early boatbuilders of the Nile were always tied to the hollow-log boatbuilding syndrome. All of their boats for nearly 2,000 years,

basically frameless and keelless, were massively planked. These planks, really log-like timbers, were assembled and keyed together with mortices, tenons, and lashings, and then shaped and fashioned. There is the evidence of old reliefs showing the ancient builders working with adzes, literally sculpting a boat. Such reliefs may possibly be artistic impressions or may be true renditions. Nevertheless, the ancient boats of Egypt progressed from bundles of reeds and simple hollowed logs to comparatively large vessels of planked bottoms and sides that carried lofty rigs and were capable of profitable trade on the sea. They were undoubtedly the first to lead in this inevitable direction. They unquestionably were the first to use edge-to-edge planking, which was, many centuries later, to be identified as the Mediterranean shipbuilding fashion and called "carvel" planking.

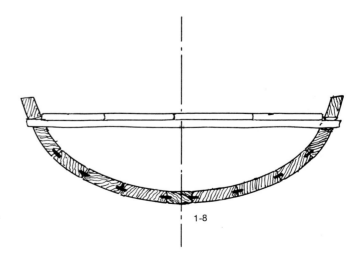

1-8

1-9   The earliest boat framing was probably much like this. These are natural-grown timbers set up for planking a West Indian sloop at Bequia, Grenadines, B. W. I.

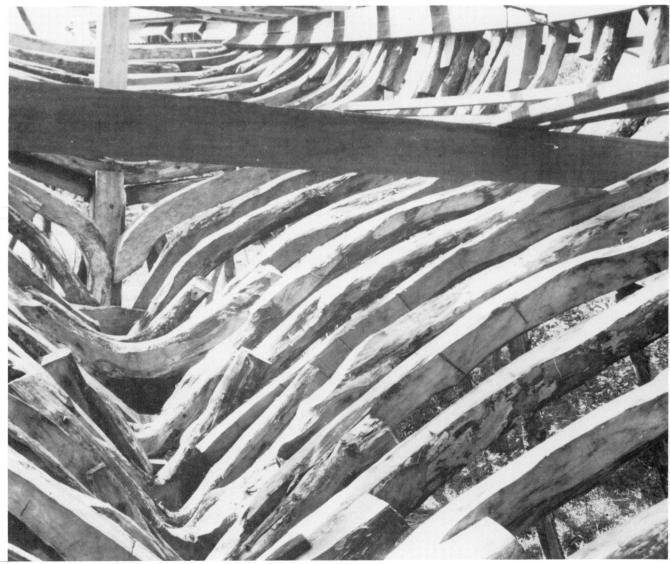

1-9

There is no direct evidence to credit the Minoans of the Aegean with the invention of the framed boat, but it is certainly a logical conclusion because their successors and the inheritors of their seagoing expertise, the Phoenicians, built boats with carvel planking on *transverse* frames. Phoenician boats too, of course, had continuous keels turning at the ends into identifiable stems.

Undersea archeology has in the last decade been quite fruitful in filling some of the gaps in the knowledge of ancient Mediterranean craft. A recent find off the coast of Turkey has revealed the intact bottom structure of a Greek trading boat of the fifth century B.C. This vessel is about 50 feet in length and about 18 feet in beam. Her bottom is framed with transverse timbers spaced from 10 to 14 inches and with intermediate frames (which may have been added after her original construction to reinforce her tired hull). The frames are about five inches by three inches on the average and are attached to the keel in the middle body by heavier floor timbers. The planking is morticed and tenoned edge to edge in the same fashion as the old frameless Egyptian boats, but the Greek boat's planks are also fastened to frames, which gives the ship a true transverse rib structure.

Most significantly there is evidence in this boat of an innovation that made possible the existence of larger and heavier vessels in the salty, teredo-infested Mediterranean. Her bottom is sheathed in one-eighth inch lead sheeting. The Minoan boats and no doubt the Phoenician boats required frequent beaching. In fact some experts believe that all of these early Aegean boats were always hauled out on the tideless beaches when not in use because of the destructive wood-boring teredo. This, in itself, would require lightly planked, framed hulls. When ultimately the boats' bottoms could be protected by lead sheathing, it no longer was necessary to beach them. They were probably hauled or careened periodically for cleaning but could at least be protected in the water for long voyages. Of such small elements as the discouragement of a sea worm is human progress made.

It was not until the early empire of the Romans, after the birth of Christ, that a conventional frame-plank structure was developed as it exists today in in the Mediterranean and much of the Western world. Here again, archeological finds of fairly intact vessels of past eras convince us beyond question of the existence of frame-plank construction.

The most notable discoveries of boats of the Roman Empire were the finds in Lake Nemi, some twelve miles southeast of Rome. Two quite large hulls were found there in 1932 when the lake was drained. The basic construction of these boats was recognizably modern, being of heavy scarfed and sawn external keel, properly spaced frames, internal keelson, double bilge stringers, deck beams with stanchion supports from the frames, and many other techniques used in the best of wood shipbuilding up to the twentieth century. These two boats of Nemi were never accurately dated or identified before fire destroyed them in World War II. Roman coins, however, were found in one boat, the most recent dated 164 A.D. It is likely that the vessels were somewhat older, for their style conforms to Roman ships of the first century A.D.

The Lake Nemi finds indicate that wooden shipbuilding had matured by the first century A.D. to the character it maintains today. Aside from comparatively minor improvements from this time on, the well-known Mediterranean style of boat construction was established. The changes to be observed in boat and ship construction were to be those of configuration, size, and performance capabilities — advances that belong to the study of ship design rather than indigenous boats.

As is obvious from the foregoing, two basic systems of boat construction have been used by western man — the Mediterranean smooth-plank-over-heavy-frame system and the Norse lapped-plank-over-light-frame system. Boats of these two basically different building systems now coexist in both Europe and America. It is interesting, however, that in the Mediterranean, where carvel construction began and was for so long the only method of building boats, the lapstrake system has never been accepted.

Today, carvel planking is used more often than lapstrake for larger and more expensive working boats in northern Europe and America. Even in Scandinavia most of the offshore fishing craft are smooth planked, though the builders of smaller boats and beach-operated boats continue logically to use the lighter, clinker construction.

The classic smooth-plank construction is unquestionably a preferable system today, where a hull of smooth, clean exterior surface is the result. With proper attention to a structural frame that includes adequate bilge stringers, uniform frames — either steam-bent, sawn from grown crooks, or doubled with futtocks — sturdy keel, keelson, clamps and shelves, and continuous deck-strengthening members, the carvel system is the ultimate in wood boat construction.

Modern carvel construction includes a certain amount of lamination in the backbone and frames, though this technique, for economy reasons, has not been adopted entirely by workboat yards. While there is much to recommend wood lamination for strength, continuity, and uniformity, it is not economical unless the builder is building a number of boats of identical model. In the great majority of boatyards or boatbuilding localities (by yards or individuals), the techniques used are still bound by experience and tradition. This is true in northern and southern Europe, the coast of Norway, and the Mediterranean. There are few people more conservative than the men who live by the sea.

It is appropriate at this point to examine the structure of a typical and traditional small working boat of the western Mediterranean. The example chosen here might well be identified as a prototype of the small beach and harbor boats of the entire western basin of the Middle Sea from Italy to Gibraltar. These boats are familiar to any traveler or vacationer in this beautiful maritime

1-10   A contemporary Aegean island fishing boat under construction. It is being carvel planked over sawn frames.

1-10

1-11

1-11 Side views of a partially planked model of a French pointu.

1-12 The structure of a modern carvel-planked boat is shown in this section of a Mediterranean beach boat of the coast of Spain. Notice the light planking, the sawn two-part frames, and the heavy keel. This boat is about the same length and beam as the ancient Sesostris boat, but its form and lightness make it much more manageable.

1-13 Looking down on the pointu model.

1-14 Mediterranean influence is apparent in this Monterey boat of the U.S. west coast. The caravel-type rub rails, dating from medieval construction, are still used here to good functional advantage.

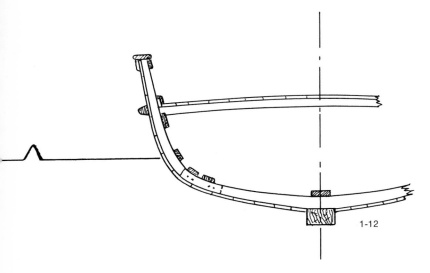

1-12

corner of the world. They vary in size from about 14 feet to as much as 30 feet. There are local preferences and deviations in form and style as noted in Chapter 5, but in basic structure they conform to a single system. They are today the living examples of and the primary heirs to the original Mediterranean carvel technology. Although, in theory, the carvel system is fundamentally the same as that which evolved finally during the flowering of the Roman Empire, the boat of today contains all of the refinements of centuries of development and use.

This Mediterranean "original" is best shown by a model, which remains unplanked to show her exquisitely fashioned structure (see Figures 1-11 and 1-13). The model is of a ubiquitous double-ended Mediterranean boat with extended stem and stern posts. The keel is straight or with a very slight rocker curve, and its sectional proportion is 1:3, sided to molded dimension. It is scarfed at both ends to the curving end posts. The frames are sawn and doubled up to the turn of the bilge, where they continue singly to the rail cap. The frame doubling in the bottom eliminates the necessity of the floor timbers required in the more common type of carvel framing and is far superior when the doublings are sawn from natural crooks. A longitudinal keelson or flat center plank placed on top of these double bottom frames and running out at the stem and stern posts completes a most rigid backbone. There are two bilge stringers per side.

This particular boat is essentially an open boat,

16

1-13

but with a deck. The deck structure can be easily seen in the illustrations. The central deck beams are actually thwarts, but the partial deck beams or carlings are "laid flat," contrary to usual western European practice. This is no doubt a concession to the open middle body of the boat, but it is typical of all Mediterranean open beach and harbor craft. The deck is "set down," and there is a deep gunwale with the open frame ends showing, having been "let" into the deck's coverboard along the waterways. There is an additional stringer or clamp below the caprail, which is a broad, flat piece finishing out to the full-molded dimension of the stem and stern posts. The caprail is finished, as is the main deck clamp below, with breast hooks — long fitted grown knees — fastened and secured to the stem and stern posts. Finally, as is the general practice, there is an unusually heavy exterior wale at the deck line to protect and stiffen the whole hull. It is on top of this wale that scuppers are cut from the deck through the lower sheer plank for drainage.

Within the Mediterranean style of boats, beyond the basic structure as illustrated and described above, there is a variety of minor, very minor, variations, aberrations, and decorations. These boats are, for example, nearly all equipped with king posts in the rail at the bow and often at the stern for snubbing mooring lines or working fishing gear. The stem heads generally are capped or carved to a distinctive profile. The stern post is frequently cut down to accommodate the tiller adequately, but not always. Often the rudder-head rises high above an already extended stern post as in the Adriatic, Maltese, and many Spanish boats.

All in all, the boat observed here in this small model is fundamental and can serve as the prototype for Mediterranean boats. Actually, it is a specific type used on the French coast near Marseilles and Toulon, and known there as a "Pointu" or sometime a "Rafiau." It is used mostly by individual fishermen or watermen and either rowed or sailed. It is of ancient, handsome construction and is a "pure" model. A typical structural midship section of this basic example is illustrated in Figure 1-12. Mediterranean-type boats can be found in faraway places, as well. The Monterey boat (see Figure 1-14), an American boat, is of pure Mediterranean construction down to its caravel wales.

1-14

The next boat to be studied is the most advanced in contemporary wood boatbuilding circles. A discussion of it provides an opportunity to illustrate the common character of boats from different ages: an excellent lesson in the persistence of man's memory and the strength of his ancient inheritance.

Boats have been built in the British Islands since Neolithic men first put together their skin coracles. The boats of the Celts and early Anglo-Saxons have developed into the most outstanding of all boats in strength and capability.

There are few boats of any of the world's maritime regions that are able to compare in construction with the better examples of the wooden fishing craft, pilot craft, or coastal working boats of Scotland, England, or Ireland.

An example of one of the best of these contemporary working boats, which is typical and indigenous enough to be identified as modern Irish-Anglo-Saxon, is the 52-foot motor fishing vessel whose structural profile and section are shown in Figure 1-15. This boat shows the common form of a rugged, heavy displacement hull typical of the modern inshore fishing craft working off the coasts of Ireland and England. Her unusually strong backbone structure should first be observed. She has a prime keel of African iroko (French Cameroons, Grade "A"), which is sided 7½" and molded 10". On top of this is an inner or hog keel of the same material that lies flat, 4½" by 10", and forms the rabbet for the 1⅝" iroko bottom planking. Tying the frame heels together across the keel

are 9" by 3¼" floor timbers, and on top of these, running from stem to stern, is a 8" by 5" keelson that is bolted through every floor timber and through the hog and outer keel with ¾" in diameter galvanized steel bolts. The main frames are sawn of English or Irish oak, as are the deck beams. The frames are sided 3¼" and molded from 6½" at the keel to 3½" at the rail. The stem, sternpost, deadwood, stringers, planking, and decks are all of iroko, which compares favorably with teak for endurance but is heavier and stronger. Iroko is considered to be the finest of boatbuilding woods for working boats where strength and durability are the primary concern.

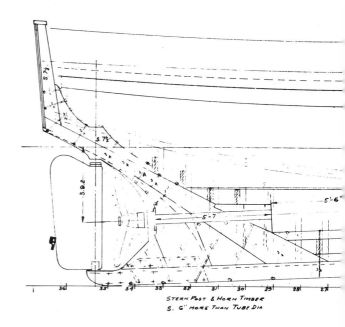

1-15 This inboard structural profile illustrates the ruggedness of a modern working boat in the Irish fisheries. She is perhaps the finest example of modern wood boat construction. Her native oak frames, many of which are natural crooks, were selected from standing trees by the builder. This is one of the rare cases where this age-old building practice is still in use.

STERN POST & HORN TIMBER
S. 6" MORE THAN TUBE DIA

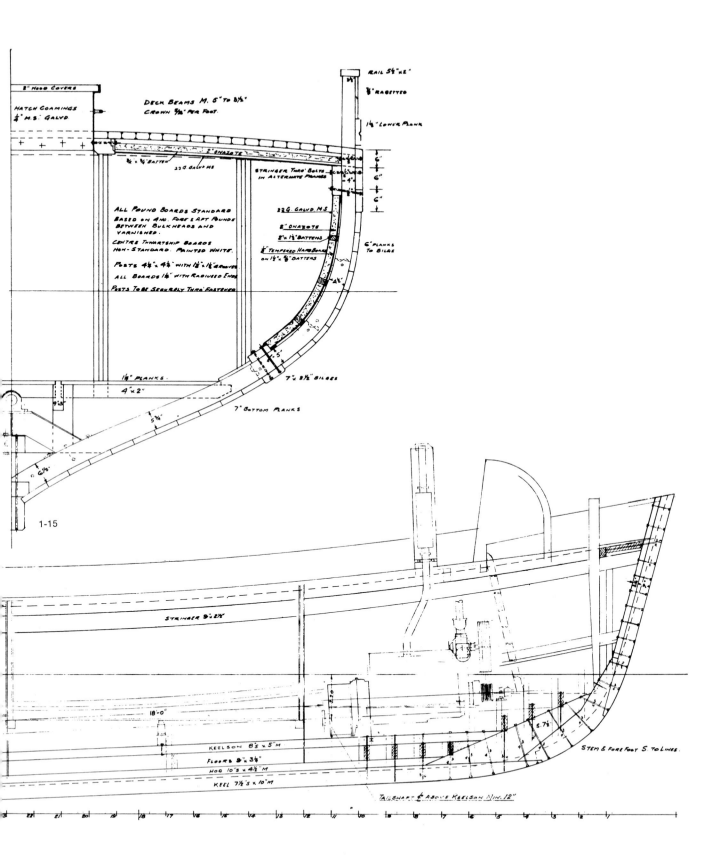

2" HOOD COVERS

HATCH COAMINGS
¾" M.S. GALVD.

DECK BEAMS M. 5" TO 3½"
CROWN 5/16" PER FOOT.

2" ONAZOTE

¾" × ¾" BATTEN

22 G GALVD MS

STRINGER THRO' BOLTS
IN ALTERNATE FRAMES

RAIL 5½" × 2"

⅜" RABBETED

1½" LOWER PLANK

6"
6"
6"
6"

32 G. GALVD. M.S.

2" ONAZOTE

8" × 1¾" BATTENS

6" PLANKS
TO BILGE

¼" TEMPERED HARD BOARD
ON 1¾" × ¾" BATTENS

ALL POUND BOARDS STANDARD
BASED ON 4 NO. FORE & AFT POUNDS
BETWEEN BULKHEADS AND
VARNISHED.
CENTRE THWARTSHIP BOARDS
NON-STANDARD. PAINTED WHITE.
POSTS 4½" × 4½" WITH 1½" × 1¾" GROOVES
ALL BOARDS 1½" WITH RADIUSED ENDS
POSTS TO BE SECURELY THRO' FASTENED

4½"

1½" PLANKS.

4" × 2"

7" × 3½" BILGES

5¾"

7" BOTTOM PLANKS

6½"

1-15

STRINGER 9" × 2½"

18'-0"

KEELSON 8"S × 5"M

FLOORS 8" × 3½"

HOG 10"S × 4½" M

KEEL 7½"S × 10"M

5.7½"

STEM & FORE FOOT S. TO LINES.

TAILSHAFT ℄ ABOVE KEELSON MIN. 12"

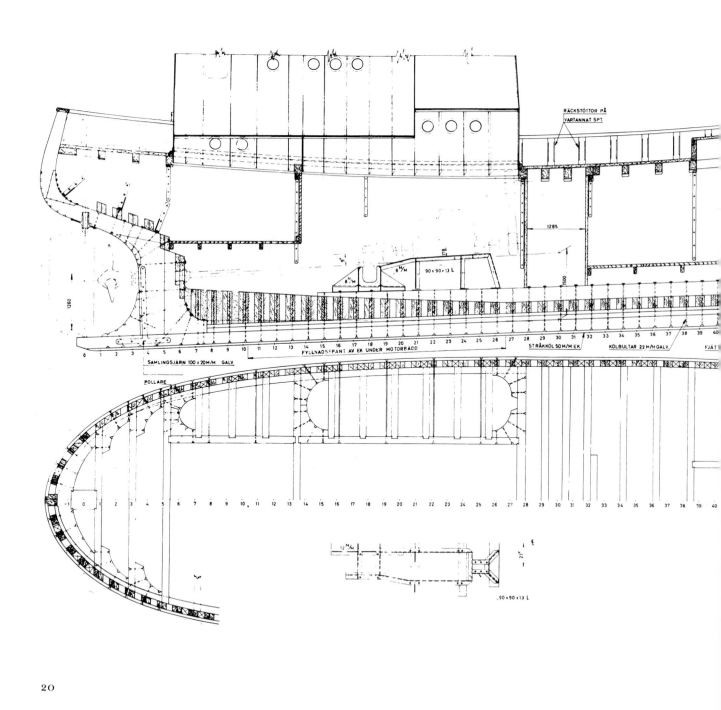

RÄCKSTÖTTOR PÅ
VARTANNAT SPT.

1285

1500

1260

90 x 90 x 13 L

8 M/M

8 M/M

SAMLINGSJÄRN 100 x 20 M/M GALV.

FYLLNADSSPANT AV EK UNDER MOTORBÄDD

STRÅKKÖL 50 M/M EK

KÖLBULTAR 22 M/M GALV.

FJÄT

POLLARE

0 1 2 3 4 5 6 7 8 9 10 11 12 13 14 15 16 17 18 19 20 21 22 23 24 25 26 27 28 29 30 31 32 33 34 35 36 37 38 39 40

-1 0 1 2 3 4 5 6 7 8 9 10 11 12 13 14 15 16 17 18 19 20 21 22 23 24 25 26 27 28 29 30 31 32 33 34 35 36 37 38 39 40

12 M/M

90 x 90 x 13 L

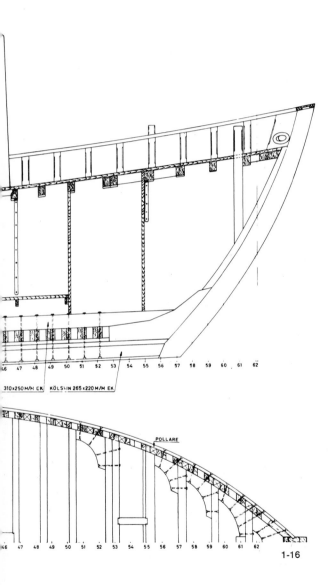

1-16

1-16 The structural profile of this Swedish trawler-seiner shows the same, fine, rugged construction evident in the Irish boat of Figure 1-15. For reasons of economy and availability, the quality of the wood is not as high as the Irish example.

The hull of this boat was assembled in the latter part of 1970 in one of the best building yards in Ireland. There is nothing in her basic structure that would be unfamiliar to the better shipwrights of 1,500 years ago. Her scarfed keel assembly with the inner log and her keelson over heavy floor timbers would have brought favorable comment from ancient Greek and Roman shipbuilders, though they would have expressed wonder over the uniformity of the structural members and the protective galvanized coatings of the steel fastenings. They might have been slightly skeptical of the lack of edge-fastening tenons in the planking, but their worries of plank security would surely have been quickly dispelled when they inspected the improved heavy, square-cut galvanized boat spikes and heavy bronze screws.

What would an ancient Viking boatbuilder think of this "best example" of twentieth century boatbuilding? He undoubtedly would complain that the boat was unnecessarily heavy for all its strength. He would see no excuse or purpose for throughbolting the floors to the frames, nor would he perhaps understand the heavy decks over beams connected to the frames. But this boat is not his style; it is of smooth plank, carvel construction, for which he would probably show contempt. Yet this same construction, even heavier still, is found in a modern Swedish boat (see Figure 1-16).

There is a structural framing variation in carvel-built boats that has been long familiar to North Americans but is finding increasing use with Northern European builders. This system employs the

1-17   Carvel planking is not always attached to sawn, pre-set frames. This boat is being carvel planked over steam-bent frames set inside a cradle-like jig. The mold is formed by setting up sectional forms that are held in place by ribbands. The hot, steamed oak frames are bent into this cradle. The ribbands are removed as the planks are fitted. The boat is the Blue Moon, designed by the author.

steam-bent frame, rather than the sawn, shaped frame. In this system, temporary molds are set up on the backbone structure and temporary heavy battens or ribbands are bent around the molds, as shown in Figure 1-17. The hot, steamed frames are then forced into shape against the inside surface of the ribbands and clamped or temporarily fastened. The planking is then attached progressively from the keel; the ribbands are removed as the planked surface proceeds. This method can be seen in progress in the photograph. The molds are finally removed when the planking is nearly completed.

The boat in Figure 1-17 was built in Norway to the basic design of a sloop of the Falmouth estuary, a boat type described in Chapter 4. She is 23 feet long with a beam of 8½ feet and draft of 4 feet. She has an oak backbone, ash frame, fir planks, and pine deck and deck beams. Her transom and rail caps are mahogany. Her mast and spars are solid, built-up spruce. Her planking is fastened to the frames by square copper rivets that are identical to the plank fastenings used by the Norwegians since the ninth and tenth century A.D.

There are newer methods of boat construction today as is known by any who are only slightly aware of the pleasure boat explosion of the 1960s. Boats of molded reinforced plastic, popularly called fiberglass, are economical only when multiple units are to be built from the same mold. There are, of course, fiberglass working boats, but they are manufactured in mass quantities to be adapted to general uses in various environments. They are hardly indigenous in character or design. It is true that in

some cases the style and form of specific indigenous working boats have been copied or synthesized in molded fiberglass boats. In such cases where this has been done for pleasure craft, the results are usually disappointing. However, new and improved working boat forms have been developed for fiberglass construction, and this rugged material has proved successful where an adequate number of boats can be built to amortize the cost of tooling. Also the use of aluminum, which is often a most expensive building material, has been very successful in some small seiners and larger shrimpers of North America. In all of these cases, the investment required in design and construction is limited to the building of large numbers of boats. It is beyond the means of the individual workboat builder who continues to build with his unique, instinctive skill borne through an experienced eye. Such a builder is free to exercise his individual creativity, but is usually restricted by his inherited conservatism and traditionalism. These contemporary builders remain but are diminishing in number. They are the source of true indigenous boats.

As mentioned previously, some of the very early methods of boatbuilding still survive, very often side by side with the most advanced techniques. This is true of the Welsh coracle and the Irish curragh, contemporary portable frame-skin boats with ancient origins in the British islands. The coracle shown in Figure 1-18 is obviously improved very

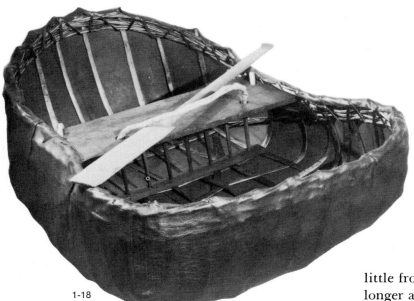

1-18

little from the original. However, the "skin" is no longer an animal's hide. It is now an impregnated canvas fabric. The frame is woven of supple green limbs that have been barked and split. The rim (it can hardly be called a gunwale or sheer clamp) is woven of small, whole willow branches, which hold the peripheral shape and provide a reinforced edge to which to lash the fabric. This craft is an elemental vessel that provides man a most basic method of buoyant support. It satisfies needs that, in some regions, have become no more demanding than they were at first. Subsequent needs, elemental as they were, produced the curragh, shown in the drawings of an Aran Island craft in Figure 1-19. The form of this skin-frame craft is here elongated to a basic boat form with a rounded stern and pointed bow for directional control. The frame consists of light, flat wood strips running both longitudinally and transversely with a heavier sheer strip containing the oar tholes. These boats are 15 to 25 feet long, but light enough to be carried overhead easily by two men. They are still used in Ireland, launched from the beach to pursue lazy but powerful basking sharks.

The dugout canoe has been referred to previously as a prehistoric boat, fundamental in design and construction. Before the dugout canoe, there were only floating logs. Yet in this age of voyages to the moon, there are still more utilitarian dugout boats in use throughout the world than any single type of boat. There are some of fine and

1-18   One of the oldest and most primitive boats. This frame-skin craft is a coracle from the River Teifi, Wales.

1-19   The Irish curragh (pronounced "corack") is the Hibernian version of the ancient Neolithic skin-frame boat. The frame of the curragh is more sophisticated, as this plan shows, and the boat has a more conventional shape.

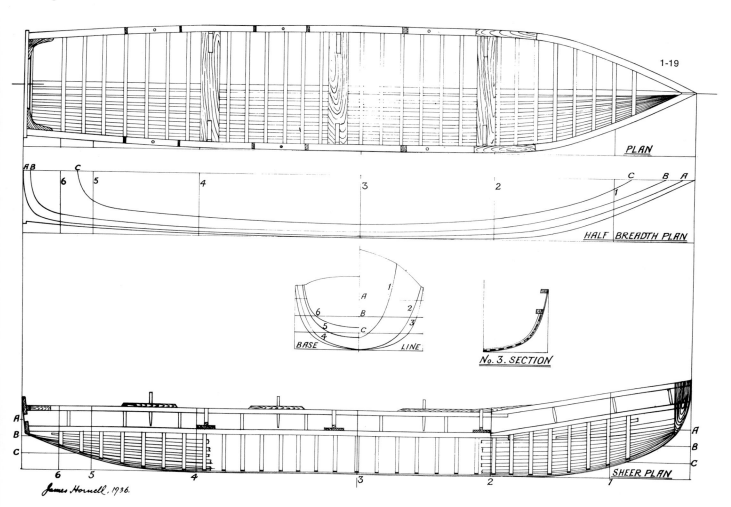

1-19

PLAN

HALF BREADTH PLAN

No. 3. SECTION

BASE   LINE

SHEER PLAN

James Hornell, 1936.

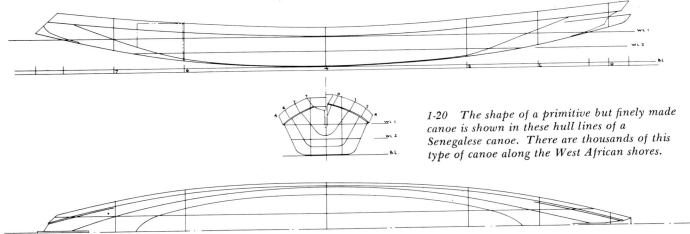

1-20 The shape of a primitive but finely made canoe is shown in these hull lines of a Senegalese canoe. There are thousands of this type of canoe along the West African shores.

1-20

sophisticated line, such as the Chesapeake sailing log canoes. These graceful over-rigged sailing craft, which originated first as simple crabbing skiffs, are now used only for the exhilarating sport of exhibition sailing and racing for pleasure. Built generally of several (up to five) logs fastened transversely, they are literally carved and sculpted into double-ended sailing hulls with fine lines, 25 to 35 feet long. They carry a large crew for live and transferable ballast on hiking boards to counter the lofty spread of sails set on their raked and unstayed masts. They are no longer working boats.

The more humble working log canoes are used in more primitive communities such as those in the Pacific islands, Caribbean islands, Indonesia, or the West African coast. They are all basically similar in size and form, since they are restricted by the workable size of tropical trees. Inasmuch as the observations of this book are concerned with the western cultures, it is the log dugouts of the West African coast that will be described.

On the coast of the African bulge, which is now the area from Nigeria to Senegal, there are more than 50,000 working dugout log boats. These boats are not river canoes, although there are many more similar dugout boats in the rivers and on the lakes of this area of Africa. The dugouts of the coastal communities are ocean-working, surf-launched boats. The fishing industry is so rewarding here that a single well-manned boat of 30 to 35 feet might be responsible for as much as 50 tons of fish per year. Approximately 90 percent of the total protein diet of the people of these coastal countries is obtained from the seafood caught from these very primitive boats.

Figures 1-20 and 1-22 illustrate the typical form of two different styles of boat, which are the basic models for many thousands. Figure 1-20 shows a Senegal beach fishing boat, and Figure 1-22 shows the type of boat used along the coast of Ghana and Dahomey. The Senegalese boat has much the same form, in the rocker-like profile and the sections, as some of the boats of ancient Egypt.

The most common length of the West African log dugout is between 25 and 30 feet with a beam of about 4½ feet. The logs are from selected large

1-21

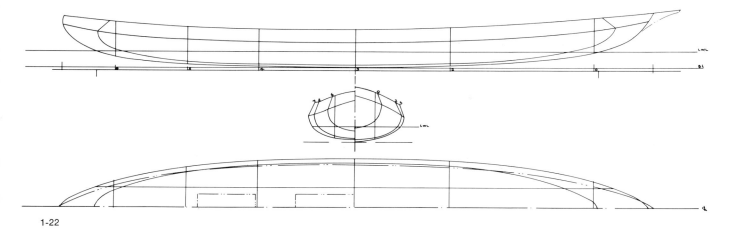

1-22

trees, often found deep in the interior as much as 150 miles from the nearest navigable water. The wood that native builders find most choice for dugouts is the best red African mahogany — prized also by the builders of the most modern yachts. The African boat "maker" uses only two tools to sculpt his boat. These tools have been used the longest in man's boatbuilding experience. The adze and a broad chisel are the cutters, shapers, and carvers of a dugout log boat, as well as of the most modern wood keel or stem post of the finest yacht. It is remarkable to observe the trueness of form that these African craftsmen achieve with these tools in the finished canoe. Some evidence of this can be seen in Figure 1-23.

The canoes of Ghana, which are more abundant than those of Senegal, have nicely rounded hulls with a rocker sheer, as can be seen in Figure 1-22. The bow and stern are almost identical in shape, though the after body is slightly fuller in the larger models. These canoes often have drawn-out stern and stem pieces that can best be described as a bill. The hulls, which are often carved by one man, require about three months' work, and are about six inches thick at the bottom and taper off to about three inches at the sheer rail. The sides show a flat in the section, which results in a tumblehome of the entire form, as well as what appears to be a continuous broad sheer strake. The seats or thwarts are often loose or sometimes fastened across the upper edges from side to side.

The boats were originally built for about six to eight paddle-wielding fishermen, which was un-

1-23

1-21   A Chesapeake log canoe. The boats were originally developed for crabbing and oystering by individual watermen, and this racing rig is not typical of the original working sails. Working log canoes often had only one mast.

1-22   The efficient form of a Ghana canoe makes it superior to the Senegal canoe. It is round-bottomed with less rocker than the Senegal canoe.

1-23   Even though they are worn and weathered, these canoes show the true shape given by the skilled use of an adze and a broad chisel.

doubtedly the prime moving system. In a few regions, however, a very simple and unstayed mast with a low-cut lugsail is used.

In recent years, the most progressive West African fishermen, through Food and Agriculture Organization aid as well as U. S. foreign aid, have been motorizing their canoes. They generally use an outboard engine of 10 to 20 horsepower mounted in a centerline well in the afterbody as shown. This simple application was first studied by model tests in towing tanks to find the most advantageous location and shape of the aperture. Such use of modern research technology has probably never before been used for the improvement of such an ancient and elemental design.

A variation in dugout form is to be found on the coast of Senegal, where these beach boats have essentially the old dory section with a flat bottom section and flared-out sides. There is also on this type the addition of a sheer plank, which serves to increase the freeboard and provides a drier hull and greater capacity.

Launching and beaching these boats has always been a haphazard procedure, which on a rough day often appears to be foolhardy or even impossible. For a dugout manned only by paddlers, it can be a most discouraging way to begin a day. The boat can capsize, pitchpole, or broach. The crew can be continually cast out of the boat. The confrontation often ends with all hands going home to forget and await a better day. Mechanization of the canoes has improved this launching operation. A motor-powered dugout's success in moving through

a surf is about 60 percent better than the paddle-propelled boat, and less crew is needed. Landing with a full load of fish in a significant surf is generally quite simple. The boat, as it approaches the line of breakers, is simply abandoned and often deliberately overturned. The crew swims ashore and picks up the fish from the beach as they roll in. Much fine fresh fish is harvested by these common boats, perhaps more than is consumed in the United States.

The Senegalese dugout, shown in Figure 1-24, is a capacious craft that, in the course of history, has advanced to the point of metamorphosis from a dugout log to a plank-sided boat. It is about 35 feet long and has a beam of about 6 feet.

Another type of primitive boat still survives, not along the edge of the sea, but in rivers and marsh-lands. This boat is made of woven and bound reeds and can be found in Lake Chad in the upper reaches of the Nile valley, in Central and South America, in the Caspian Sea marshes, and undoubtedly in other remote regions where primitive people live marginally. This form of watercraft was used in the pre-dynastic eras of ancient Egypt. It has been used continually since, especially where men are considerably restricted by the adversaries of poverty, poor agriculture, and shallow wetlands.

In the emerging society of ancient Egypt, the reed boat or papyrus raft was fashioned carefully with a boat shape. Papyrus reeds were abundant, and consequently the craft were cheap, popular

1-24

1-24   A Senegalese log canoe returning with a small catch of fish. Note the planked-up sides of this dugout hull, living evidence of one step in the evolution of the planked boat.

means of flotation for fishing and hunting in the marshes. These boats were and are extremely perishable, lasting about a month to six weeks when used regularly. They were consequently made to be disposable and economically replaceable. The early Egyptians apparently made craft of papyrus reeds much in the same way as they are made today in the region of Lake Chad. They also apparently made them quite large, perhaps as much as 50 to 60 feet. It would be a considerable extension of logic, however, to reason that such craft were ever used beyond the rivers. The gradual absorption of water and subsequent waterlogging, combined with chafe from the motion of the sea, to say nothing of the unwieldiness of such a hulk as it loses its shape, would be convincing evidence of its lack of suitability for moving on saltwater seas such as the Mediterranean.

In summary, it is obvious that primitive man built watercraft of whatever materials were close at hand, wherever he lived. As he gained some mobility from these first craft, he provided himself with better materials and improved his structural techniques to provide a craft of even greater mobility. Such progress in boat design and construction made civilization possible.

2 / NORTH AMERICAN WORKING CRAFT

AMERICAN CULTURE is comparatively young — only a few hundred years old. Because of this, the great works of our artists, writers, and craftsmen are relatively few in number. In addition, much of our culture is not original, but is directly adopted or at least reflected from European origins, particularly in the more humble crafts and skills. With such limitations, it is remarkable that Americans developed a true indigenous culture in many diversified arts and skills in various separated localities. The shipbuilding skills, as well as all of the maritime arts, are a rich source of American culture. The present leadership of the United States in world affairs owes much to this turn of Yankee ingenuity.

In my concern with the small indigenous workboats of North America, I have been discriminating. In the wide scope of present-day working craft along the thousands of miles of North America's coastline and within the boundaries of maritime provinces and coastwise states, there are some craft that are copies of Old World boats or directly reflect such heritage. These European adaptations cannot reasonably be included as true American craft. Such examples may be noted briefly, but their truer and less adulterated ancestors are still likely to exist and thus will be described in their original environment in later chapters.

It would be unwise and unfair to plunge directly into descriptions of existing American boats without first paying respect to those most worthy craft that have passed into extinction with the days of sail. Along the eastern seacoast of North America, from the Canadian provinces to the Gulf of Mexico, during the nineteenth century, large numbers of sailing workboat types were in use. Most of these craft were purely American in design and construction. Many survived into the early twentieth century, but almost all have gone today. The causes of their extinction are obvious and well documented. For the most part, the advantages and attractions of mechanical propulsion made sail uneconomical. The expansion of the American economy and the technologies of mechanical refrigeration, rapid transportation, and urbanization of society were also equal contributors to the extinction of these fine old sailing craft.

Many truly American sailing craft were significant and deserve mention. The early colonial and Revolutionary War sloops and shallops developed and evolved into schooner types. Some of the most notable were built in Chesapeake Bay and loosely referred to as Baltimore schooners. On the New England coast the old heel-tapper fishing schooners gave way to the faster and seaworthy pinky schooners and larger Banks schooners as fishing grounds were extended. The Virginia pilot schooners and New York pilot schooners of the nineteenth century became the models for later ships and yachts. The smaller double-ended schooners, such as the Block Island boats and the Chebaco boats, were fine sea-keeping models. The oyster industry of the Delaware and Chesapeake Bays developed unique craft, such as the Delaware sloop, and the Chesapeake pungy. The latter had the sleekness of a Baltimore clipper's hull. Later the Chesapeake bugeye and skipjack dominated the oyster fishery, numbering over 1,000 sail.

The smaller sloops of note along the New England coast were the double-ended Quoddy boat and the Friendship and Muscongus sloops. There were catboats developed for the scallop fisheries of the sounds, and the Noank sloop mainly for lobstering in Long Island Sound. Farther south, there were the sprit-rigged sloops of the North Carolina sounds, which were finely modeled hulls for shoal-water fishing. There were the beamy sponge sloops and smacks of Key West carrying great spreads of sail. (These should not be confused with the Greek sponge boats that later dominated this Florida fishery.) In the Gulf there were the Louisiana oyster sloops, Biloxi catboats for shrimp fishing, and the New Orleans lugger, which was said to be fast and weatherly and the only American working boat using the lug rig.

On the Pacific Coast the boats of the Columbia River and Puget Sound were smaller than the Eastern boats, were double-ended, often undecked, and carried a single sprit sail. Some of these boats were used in the gill net and salmon fisheries until very recently. The sailing workboats in the San Francisco area were direct copies of Mediterranean craft, identical in rig and hull to those of Italy and Spain. They were called by the likely but incorrect name, fellucas. A genuine felluca was a Mediterranean boat of the Algerian coast during the eighteenth and early nineteenth centuries. It was often used in the pirate business, hence its name, to

Americans, became notoriously linked with the Mediterranean.

The culmination in performance, grace, and fishing capacity of sailing workboats was finally reached in the great schooners sailing out of Boston, Gloucester, and Nova Scotia. The racing competition between these boats became so heated that the last ones built were designed by well-known yacht designers.

However gracefully these boats may have expired, they are gone and have settled for their spot in American maritime history. However profitable they may have been in their time, they could not have continued or existed in today's economy. The work of a dozen sailing lobster boats is done by one today. A fishing schooner from the Banks often arrived with rotted fish in her holds — today's modern boats do not. Today's scallop dragger can take in one haul of her dredge two days' catch for a scallop boat under sail. And most modern shrimp boats are part of multi-million dollar fleets and industries owned by very large companies.

What still attracts the individual sailor in his own small boat to the sea? There is little question that the fisherman of today in his small powerboat has faced the same diminishing opportunities as the fisherman of the past with his sailing boat. The expedience and reliability of the contemporary motor-powered workboat in some environments, however, does allow the continuance of small, individually operated craft in a competitive market.

*2-1   The unique form and lapstrake hulls of
Nova Scotian boats reflect the ancestry of
northern Europe.   This boat on the beach at
Sydney, Nova Scotia, is used by independent
fishermen in the local lobster industry.*

The coasts of northeastern America used to
abound with types of small craft that were unique
and indigenous to their regions. The majority of
these types have not been replaced after they deteriorated and consequently today only a few remain.
However, as is obvious in the ensuing chapters, indigenous craft stubbornly survive and prevail in
the more isolated communities, especially those
with significant fishing industries.

On the farther east coasts of the North American
continent, which include the maritime provinces of
Canada, the native boats are ruggedly distinguished
and flavored by their North European heritage.
Yet this is mainly just a flavor. The boats are
reminiscent of Scottish and Scandinavian craft in
their structure, which is predominantly lapstrake,
but their styles are creatively American-Nova Scotian. The general style, rather than the design, of
these boats is the indigenous factor. There are
long, slim clinker-built lobsterboats with broad
transom sterns that appear to be second cousins of
the Jonesport boat (the well-known Maine lobsterboat type to be discussed later in this chapter).
There are double-ended lapstrake pulling boats
whose form is like the timeless Norway skiffs.
There are canoe-sterned, clinker-built powerboats
that are obviously descended from the nineteenth
century small double-ended Tancook whalers or
Hampton whalers, and many others. The nineteenth century ancestors of these boats can only be
examined through their drawings and pictures; the
present day versions are still on beaches and in
harbors of Prince Edward Island and Nova Scotia.

2-1

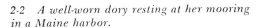
2-3

2-2   *A well-worn dory resting at her mooring in a Maine harbor.*

2-3   *Shooting a seine from a dory. Dories are rowed from either the seated or the standing position.*

2-4   *A typically shapely Maine peapod. This indigenous double ender is quite similar to some Mediterranean beach boats.*

2-5   *The capacity of a dory is surprising. The more weight she takes on, the more she will resist immersing her hull and the greater will be her stability. This one has a load of wet nets that weighs nearly half a ton.*

When I was a boy of 12, an old and skilled boat-builder friend of mine created a 14-foot sloop for me, which he built entirely by an instinctive hand. He was from Prince Edward Island, and he built from memory a handsome little lapstrake boat with steam-bent frames and a Scottish-Norse stem on molds shaped entirely by his inner eye. This boat followed me for more than 25 years, and I well remember how she was built, how I learned to sail in her, and how she responded better than any of the dozen or so boats I have owned since.

Much has been written of the New England dory and the famous Banks dory of the same mold and origin. Most observers would say that the dory is an indigenous New England type, and so it is in a way. But in another sense, a dory is built on a model that is so fundamental and natural that it is hard for any age to claim it. The first planked boats of ancient Egypt were built to this same basic form. Boats in Scotland and in southern France identified with the European Middle Ages have been of this form. There is a recent Marseille dory still in limited use almost identical to the New England dory except for the latter's "tombstone stern." A log dugout canoe used by the fishermen of the coast of Senegal in West Africa has the same basic shape. The dory form is popular and basic beyond a doubt, and it is easily identified. Its popularity stems from its natural simplicity. The sides of dory-type boats are essentially "developable," that is, they can be sprung to shape from a flat surface. A straight plank bent in an arch and set on an angle can become a dory side. The most common

2-2

2-4

2-5

nd simple dory can be built with one-piece sides. The bottom is flat with a slight rocker, and the umber of frames is minimal, perhaps only four. A more shaped and refined dory may have as many s five or six planks per side.

The dory is, to use a New Englander's description, "cranky" when light, but gains in stability as he is loaded. It established a reputation for seaworthiness as a line-trawling boat for the old Banks schooners of the nineteenth century. Quantities of ories could be carried compactly on deck in a nest" when the thwarts were removed. These oats averaged about 18 feet in length on the American schooners. The dory is in use today in eining operations. A smaller, one-man dory is sed by the contemporary Portuguese craft fishing he Grand Banks.

Another well-known and efficient little boat of New England still surviving with some vigor is the Maine peapod. This little double-ender is smaller nd more refined than a dory. The peapod was riginally designed for sailing with a small sprit il. The entire rig with mast and sprit was easily ut up or down and stowed in the boat. A peapod similar in form and size to some French Mediterranean beach boats, but without extended stem and ern posts (see Figure 2-4).

One theory is that the Maine peapod originated the Penobscot Bay region of Maine sometime in he middle of the nineteenth century. Another heory is that these little double-enders are related o or inspired by the American Indian's canoe. Both of these theories are dubious. There has al-

ways been an abundance of small double-ended hull forms in the "down east" region, which includes especially the Maritime Provinces of Canada and the Cape Breton area. These hull forms are many and varied: deep and full, shallow and light, either plumb ended or with raking ends, and either smooth planked or clinker planked. The contemporary Maine peapod also shows many of these variations in form and structure. If there is any single regional source of these double-enders, it is more likely some part of Nova Scotia. The Scots centuries ago learned to appreciate double-ended craft from the Norse.

At any rate, the Maine peapod is a serviceable little utility boat that became popular a century ago as an able little lobster-pot hauler in the Penobscot region. Peapods are still popular and can be found in various sizes, shapes, and construction forms. On several stretches of the northeast American coast, there are small double-ended utility boats from 10 to 17 feet in length. They are ideal beach boats, simple harbor boats, or tenders.

Along the coasts of northeast United States and the Maritime Provinces of Canada, there is a strong seagoing heritage. Sailboats of the past and powerboats of the present have always been built with a keen eye to both performance and ruggedness. They have been manned and owned by discriminating sailors and fishermen with demanding requirements. These boats have been built in an

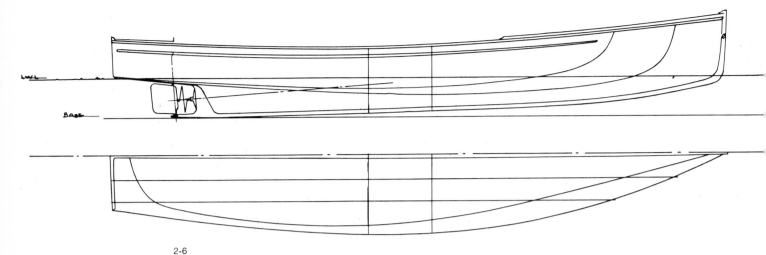

2-6

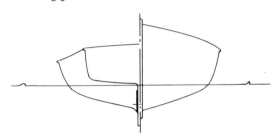

2-7

area that is near inshore and offshore fishing grounds that produce premium seafood products: lobster, scallops, and some shrimp. This area is dotted with naturally protected harbors and coves and is blessed with indigenous boatbuilding woods in fair supply. In just such an environment, boats of strong regional influence are developed. Boats built here have had a considerable influence on uncounted pleasure and working craft along the entire eastern seaboard.

As the old pinky schooners and the excellent smaller sailing craft, such as the Friendship and Muscongus Bay sloops, ended their working days, a powerboat was developed for lobster fishing in Nova Scotia that became a basic model for various similar types in both Canada and Maine. This boat in "down east" Maine was known as the *Jonesport* boat and in Nova Scotia as the *Cape Island* boat (see Figure 2-6). Her typical dimensions of length were from 32 to 45 feet, beam 10 to 12 feet, and draft (light) 2½ to 3½ feet. With her converted automobile engine she made speed up to 16 knots. She had, as her present-day version have, a fine, sharp entrance with a long, flat run of underbody terminating in a broad, flat transom. Originally, the Jonesport boat had a forefoot cut away, raking up at about 15° from the straight keel line to the stern. This made beaching easier where docking facilities or piers were not available. The construction was of light, steam-bent frames of oak or ash, closely spaced and of rather flat section. The Jonesport boat was, as most are today, planked with white cedar or sometimes clear-grade pine about 1 to 1¼ inches thick.

2-8

There was generally a low cuddy cabin forward on these partially decked boats and today invariably a steering shelter house, open on the back and at least one side, for tending the lobster haul. This shelter is often fitted with side curtains rigged for inclemencies.

In Nova Scotia, similar boats can be found that relate more closely to older sailing models with double-ended form or canoe-type sterns. The Canadian boats are sometimes undecked without any shelter.

There is no such thing as a single, stereotyped design for lobsterboats any more than there is one for most other indigenous boat types.

The contemporary Maine lobsterboats exist in many models and a variety of sizes. They reflect, to a great extent, the affluence (or lack of it) of their owners. Some are apt to be rather "hand-hammered" looking. On the other end of the scale, there are those of most modern construction and professional finish including, currently, one well-respected builder's product in fiberglass. A selection of this variety in finish and taste can be seen in Figures 2-7, 2-8, and 2-9. While these boats show individuality — they vary in size, equipment, construction quality, and in some cases hull form — they exhibit a definite overall similarity that unmistakably stamps them as a native type.

Having described the older Jonesport models, it is useful to describe similarly a very recent boat built in Blue Hill, Maine. This boat is a most excellent example of modern working-boat design in this locality. Even though the more conserva-

2-9

2-6   The lines of a Jonesport boat.

2-7   A lobsterboat of the Penobscot. This boat is not far removed from the earliest Jonesport, or Cape Island, boat. Note her side sheathing for protection where the pots are hauled aboard and the open section of her wheelhouse on the working side.

2-8   A wide variety of styles is evident in these lobsterboats at anchor.

2-9   A newly built lobsterboat on the ways.

2-10

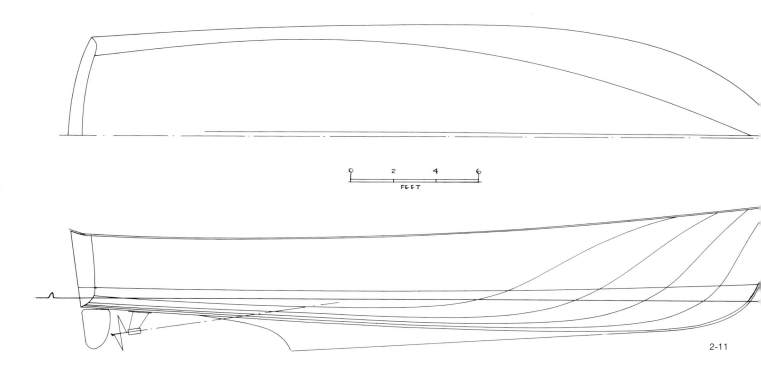

2-11

2-12

tive fishermen may still distrust her fiberglass hull, she is a very respectable example of the best in lobsterboats. (The boat is illustrated in Figure 2-10 and her lines are shown in Figure 2-11.)

First it is only fair to say that this boat was not designed in Maine but in Maryland. However, her designer was strongly influenced by the Maine model and the requirements there, and the boat does not depart from the New England form. She cannot be identified as anything other than a Maine lobsterboat. The hull is 33′10″ in length, 11′0″ in beam, and 2′6″ in draft. Her light displacement is about 7,500 pounds and she has a top speed of about 21 knots with a 170 h.p. diesel. The photograph shows her rigged for dragging, which is the off-season employment of some lobsterboats from November through March. While this model has an excellent hull form, which is quite adaptable to the requirements of the industry, she is not typical of the higher performance lobsterboats. She is not particularly fine at the waterline: her half-entrance angle is approximately 25°, while 10° to 15° is more common in the older boats and certainly permits a more easily driven hull. In addition, this hull, following the more recent tendency, shows a greater immersion at the transom. These fuller-bodied characteristics undoubtedly provide a more stable working platform and one that can carry a greater range of loads with less change in power requirements.

Leaving this analysis, it is appropriate to look briefly at some characteristics of a lobster hull model from the Portland, Maine, area. The lines of this boat are shown in Figure 2-13 and a photograph of her test model in Figure 2-12. This boat, according to her builder, was "one of several to the same molds." She "made a clean natural drift" according to one expert observer, averaging about 13 knots with a 100 h.p. converted gas engine. She shows the slack bilges of the Jonesport model and a very fine entrance with a half angle of about 10°, essentially a hollow waterline. Her length is the same as the fiberglass model described above, but she is less beamy. She is deeper in the forefoot and should be easier in a seaway. Her sections forward show a nice flare. This hull was tested, together with a number of other models of Maine lobsterboats and Chesapeake crabbing and oyster launches of similar dimensions, in the U. S. Naval Academy model basin a few years ago. This model of a Portland-built boat exhibited a clear superiority over the others as being the most easily driven. On a per-pound basis of boat weight, she showed the lowest power requirement over the complete displacement speed range. In tank tests among waves in a head-sea condition, this model again showed a definite superiority over the other models.

While the boat's tank tests described above were limited to a specific design under specific comparative power and sea-state test conditions, the model's design was exceptionally good. Her characteristics were chosen so she could be used under difficult and demanding operating conditions that require optimum stripped-hull performance. She is not a builder's all-purpose hull that can be adapted easily to a six-berth cruising yacht or to the luxury re-

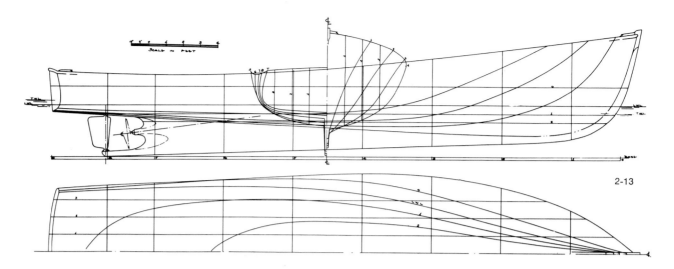

2-13

quirements of a sport-fishing boat. She is a plain and simple product embodying much of the character of an original Jonesport boat.

There is no excess weight on a good lobsterboat hull. There are no concessions or compromises in design or construction to provide roomy accommodations, or, as in many fishing craft, large fish holds, or auxiliary machinery for refrigeration. The primary employment of a lobsterboat is quite different from other fishing craft. The greatest load one must carry is a deckload of lightweight lobster pots, and even that is only intermittent. The catch of lobsters may on a very good day run to three hundred pounds, but not very often. It is not surprising, then, that the performance qualities of a lobsterboat, developed in an excellent testing environment, have attracted the attention of many small boat designers. Lobsterboat hull forms and dimensions have been widely adapted and imitated —sometimes successfully, but often with indifferent or even poor results. Where the employment of such hull types is in pleasure-craft use, there should be considerable attention given to weight limitation. Such lightweight hulls with slack bilges do not respond to great changes of displacement. Fuller entrances, greater immersions aft, higher freeboards, and harder bilges are generally the features found in the modifications to the original forms. These are all concessions for comfort, carrying capacity, and certain aspects of stability and steering.

There is also on the coast of Maine a boat that is characteristic of a broader spectrum of New Eng-

land working boats of the fisheries. This boat, while it appears from not too far a distance to be a New England-type dragger (to be discussed immediately following), is not a dragger or even a fishing boat. It is actually a fish carrier, specifically a sardine carrier. Because of its employ, it is not, nor need it be, built as ruggedly or heavily as a real working "dragger" or trawler. The Maine sardine carrier transports the produce of the fishermen to the buyers and packers. It is essentially a coastwise boat, but since it works off a northern, rugged coast from early spring to December, it is a boat built to exacting specifications to provide substantial sea-keeping ability.

On the average, these boats are 55 to 60 feet in length, with a beam of nearly 15 feet and a draft of about 5 feet. While there are some with transom or squared-off sterns, the more typical stern form is the canoe- or trawler- type. The profile and waterline form of a typical sardine carrier are shown in Figure 2-15. The strong characteristics of a high bow with an easy entrance and a dragged keel line are evident in this boat. This style of fish carrier is also seen in Figure 2-14; which shows one working out of Rockland, Maine.

Sardine carriers have especially strong bottom construction because of the concentrated loads from their built-in concrete fish tanks, whose typical capacity runs to about 1,000 bushels of sardines. Separated fish tanks in the larger of these boats provide some additional advantages to the owners and packers. For instance, the catches of different fishermen may be separated; entire loads are sel-

2-14

2-13   *The hull lines of a highly efficient lobsterboat built in Portland, Maine.*

2-14   *A sardine carrier underway.*

2-15   *The profile and waterline form of a Maine sardine carrier.*

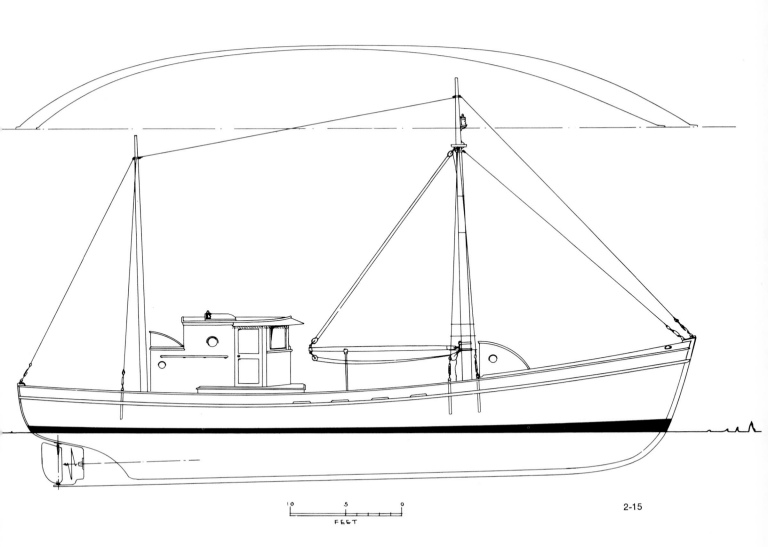

10   5   0
FEET

2-15

2-16 An eastern-rigged New England dragger. The masts can carry steadying sails. The eastern dragger, and her western sister, almost always carries at least one dory on top of, or near, the wheelhouse.

2-17 This western-rigged New England dragger is actually a combination boat. Her bow pulpit may be used for swordfishing.

2-18 A large, modern steel dragger. She still bears a strong resemblance to the original eastern type.

2-19 A Gloucester fishing schooner that has been converted to a dragger.

2-17

2-16

2-18

2-19

dom lost or condemned because of a few bad fish; and partial loads may be carried without involving the labor of cleaning a single, large, fish hold. The engine power installed in these boats varies, but 150 h.p. in a diesel is considered quite ample.

In character the sardine carrier of Maine is most traditionally "down east." While the illustrations shown are of a type, the boats vary in size and stern form, a few even in hull form. There is still, however, strong adherence to a singleness of character and style. This style is of New England. It will be seen again in the appearance and character of the dragger, a description of which follows.

The New England dragger is perhaps more indigenous to New England as a tradition than as a specific type of boat. The modern New England dragger is essentially a heavily powered fishing trawler, distinguished by its ruggedness as necessitated by its all-season operation on the exposed Georges Bank 100 miles or more beyond Cape Cod. Its design follows the modern concept of a motor trawler (a typical one being about 80 feet in length), and this concept is not indigenous to New England. Today's new boats are the sophisticated products of the most competent naval architects specializing in fishing boat design. However, there are a few of the older, smaller draggers still about New Bedford, Stonington, Gloucester, and other harbors of southern New England. These draggers reflected at least some of the characteristics of their local sailing ancestors, notably the Cape Cod catboat, Noank sloop, and Gloucester sloop boat.

There were originally two types (and many still are working) of New England draggers, the "eastern" and the "western." The essential difference in style aside from minor variations in form is the location of the deckhouse and the number of masts and their locations. The western-style dragger has the deckhouse and accommodations, including the engine space, forward and the fish hold aft. It also has a squared-off stern and a single mast. The eastern model is opposite in respect to the location of the deckhouse and the fish hold. It has two masts in a cut-down schooner arrangement.

The boats are very heavily built, with sawn frames on doubled keels and keelsons, inner and outer stems, and heavy planking. This construction follows closely nineteenth century New England shipbuilding practice which is most commendable. When such construction is used on craft smaller than the great clippers, packets, or Gloucester schooners, the boats seem to be overscaled and overweight. However, it is difficult to argue against success, and these boats have been successful. I have not seen any recorded loss of one of these draggers that was due to failure of her basic structure. They are stable and most sea-kindly.

Figures 2-16 and 2-17 show two typical New England draggers of the western and eastern styles respectively. These boats represent an intermediate stage in the evolution of the modern steel trawler (see Figure 2-18). They represent the classic mental picture conjured up when the term "New England dragger" is used on the eastern seaboard.

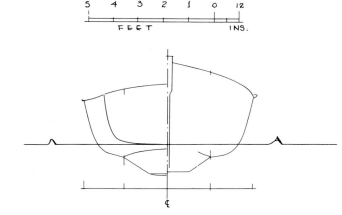

```
5   4   3   2   1   0   12
        F E E T          I NS.
```

¢

2-20

Along the coast between New England and the Chesapeake Bay, there are few noteworthy boat types that are uniform either in style or in performance. Descendants of a type known as the *Jersey sea skiff*, however, do operate from the various inlets along the New Jersey shore. The present-day models of this type have many of the qualities of good Maine lobsterboats. They have a lively sheer, flaring bow, a forward-reaching stern, and slack bilges. They are also of lightweight, but strong, construction. They generally have lapstrake planking and greater beam than most lobsterboats.

A special form of boat, called the *Seabright skiff*, can be seen occasionally along the Jersey shore. This boat is identified by its unusual bottom construction. It is essentially a round or sometimes V-bottom hull with a hollow box-type keel. This is apparent in the simple hull-form sketch of Figure 2-20. The true purpose of this appendage or distended bottom configuration is elusive. Some observers contend it allows a flat bottom surface to keep the boat upright when it is beached. Others feel it provides added bottom strength without too much added weight. It also provides a more accessible bilge under the engine, by acting as a bilge sump.

The box keel form similar to that of the Seabright skiff is, from the hydrodynamic point of view, a poor idea. It is simply an additional small hull carried below the main hull. In addition to the frictional and eddy drag it adds, the box keel is close enough to the surface to contribute to the wave drag as well. In towing-tank tests I undertook

2-20 *The lines form of the Seabright skiff.*
This lapstrake boat evolved into the powerful
sport-fishing and pleasure craft that are all
loosely labeled "sea skiffs." Note the box keel.

several years ago on several models of this type, it was most evident that this type of configuration suffered an added drag of approximately 20 to 25 percent over hulls of similar shape but without boxed keel forms. The effect on both maneuverability and power expended is nearly that to be expected if a beer keg were attached to the boat's bottom.

It is this sort of individual expression in locally conceived boats that sometimes contributes to their early extinction. The survival of Seabright skiffs for their 50 years or more is undoubtedly due to other qualities. Their lightness and strength, as well as comparative dryness, are important factors. However, I suspect that some of the larger models, which were highly powered during the Prohibition Era of the 1920's, earned an exaggerated reputation for evasiveness in a sub-rosa world.

The Chesapeake Bay area is a unique body of tidal water. Its ecology nurtures a great abundance and variety of seafood. Its channels and tributaries lead close to many large urban areas. Quite naturally the Bay has large numbers of workboats working profitably between its shores.

Most of the Chesapeake Bay boats of considerable distinction in the days of sail no longer exist. A fleet of sailing workboats still exists, however, that is most notable — more notable perhaps for the unique survivability of the fleet than for the qualities of the individual boats.

Before describing these sailing workboats, it may be pertinent to note briefly the employment available to these working boats of Chesapeake Bay.

The fisheries in temperate zones generally provide a seasonal industry. The Chesapeake is a good example of this natural cyclic employment. Fortunately, there is a variety of seafood available for harvesting, and the employment seasons also extend themselves nearly throughout the year. In the summer months, from early May through September, the crabbing season is in force. Beginning in October and extending through April, the oyster season goes on. Clams are taken by hydraulic dredge throughout the year but are better during the colder seasons. There are no other shellfish to be found commercially in the Bay. The fish are most important in late winter, spring, and fall.

In addition to the fisheries, there is a certain amount of cargo and produce still moved on the water by small carriers. Some of these carriers serve the fisheries and other commercial and farm needs.

It is remarkable that in this industrial, agricultural, and maritime region there are no more indigenous boat types than there are. This is true perhaps because the watermen and owners of working boats employ themselves in more than a single industry and use the same boats for more than a single purpose.

The most common type of boat construction in the Chesapeake Bay is the shoal V-bottom hull known locally as a *deadrise*. This term is a generic one and does not adequately describe any boat. It is perhaps better to briefly describe a typical Chesa-

2-21 A Chesapeake Bay buy boat loaded down with a deckload of oysters.

2-22 This curve indicates the distribution of hull volume for a typical deadrise boat. The greatest volume occurs at about 35 percent of the boat's length from the stern.

2-23 The hull form of a typical Chesapeake round-stern deadrise. This type of boat may be seen in Maryland and Virginia waters of the bay in many sizes and occupations, from small oyster-tonging boats to large buy boats.

peake fishing launch as a chine-built boat of from 30 to 45 feet in length, 8½ to 11 feet in beam, and 3 to 4 feet in draft, with a shallow V bottom ending on a chine slightly below the waterline. The chine is low and flat throughout, rising only slightly forward sometimes above the waterline. The stem is generally plumb or raked a little forward, but almost always has a straight stem post. The sterns are round with a graceful rake aft or have a flat transom with little or no rake. The round-stern boats are generally the larger ones and are used most frequently as oyster tongers with patent tongs. The smaller square-stern boats are used in shallower waters, and during the oyster season they are operated by one man with the old-style hand tongs.

Actually, the powered launches of the upper and lower Bay are all variations on a single theme. They vary primarily in size, and regional and seasonal employment. As the old sailing brogans were smaller, open editions of the bugeyes, the small power launches are similar to the large ones and, even in basic form, to the larger light-freight carriers and many "buy boats." They may rig clam dredges in spring and summer, and then rig the mast-boom rig for lifting the heavy patent tongs in the fall and winter. A buy boat is a large deadrise 50 to 70 feet long that is capable of carrying upwards of 25 tons of oysters, which are bought from the oystermen in the Bay or before the oystermen return to port (see Figure 2-21).

Figure 2-23 shows the lines of a typical round-stern launch, and Figure 2-24 shows those of a smaller square-stern model. The form of this latter boat indicates a lighter, more easily driven boat. However, her low forward chine and full entrance do not indicate that she would be very competitive among the finer hulls of the New England coast. In spite of her clean run aft, her low chine forward creates a shoulder wave that is inefficient and awkward. Some similar models are even fuller than this one in the forward chine.

It is in the afterbody and run of some of the larger boats that the most serious difficulties lie. The boats when under construction are set up with the keel laid horizontally along the ground blocks and the chine carried aft paralleling this horizontal keel line until (at approximately three-quarters of the waterline length) it is turned back up toward the stern waterline. This sort of chine curvature creates a full body too far aft and generates a form that is most inefficient. The distribution of displacement is such that about 60 percent of it is confined to only 20 percent of the length of the hull and that being too far aft. This displacement distribution is most evident when the curve of the sectional areas, as shown in Figure 2-22, is examined. A curve such as this simply shows the areas of the hull's cross sections below the waterline at any indicated station along the length of the hull. A hull whose characteristics are of this nature tends to have a great eddy drag as well as a considerable wave resistance.

Not all of the Chesapeake-type hulls have this extreme chine curvature. There are many that show a cleaner or flatter run, particularly the

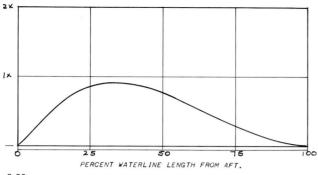

2-22

2-24   There are many variations of the square, or transom, stern deadrise, but this hull form shows a typical one. The boat is generally smaller than the round-stern deadrise and is used for crabbing and oystering. When used for oystering in the winter, this boat's two-man crew tongs the hard way with hand tongs.

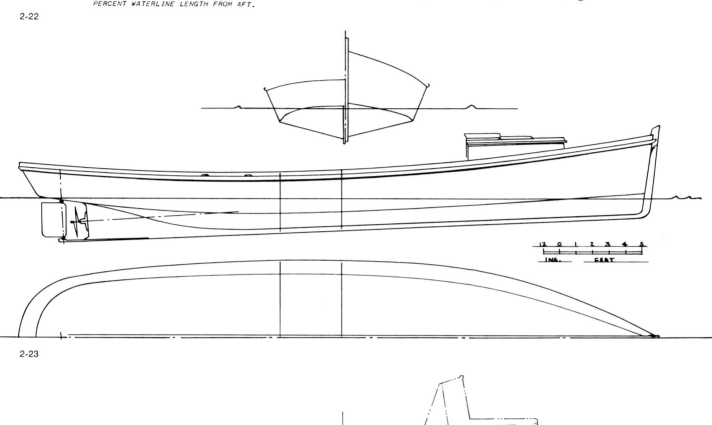

2-23

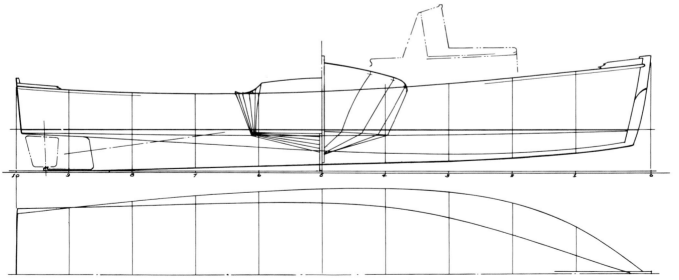

2-24

2-25 *Hand tongers at work on a square-stern deadrise.*

2-26 *The hull form of a Hooper's Island boat shows a narrow, fine-lined shape with the chine lying flat on the waterline from stem to stern. These boats are unquestionably fast and efficient in the short, choppy waves of the Chesapeake.*

2-27 *A Hooper's Island deadrise. Easily identified by its reverse-raked, rounded stern, this indigenous type is no longer being built. A substantial but diminishing number still exists in Maryland and Virginia.*

smaller craft, and these are probably the present-day descendants of the once popular and fast crabbing launch known as the *Hooper's Island boat.* The original Hooper's Island craft were characterized by a long, rather narrow hull of light weight and draft. They frequently had a rounded fantail stern with a reverse rake and a chine that followed the waterline throughout the length of the boat. The deeper sections, with sharper, "Vee's," were forward of amidships, which produced a clean, flat hull run to the transom; some boats even showed a slight hollow in the run. These boats, developed more than fifty years ago, were modeled on an early racing motorboat that appeared about 1905. This motorboat undoubtedly made a considerable impression among the Chesapeake watermen and set a style that, with further development and better engines, became a type. A typical Hooper's Island boat is shown in Figures 2-26 and 2-27; her dimensions are 35'6" length, 6'5" beam, and 2'0" draft. The boats of this early type were generally very narrow with breadths at the waterline less than one sixth of their lengths. They were consequently fast with the comparatively low-powered engines of forty years or more ago. As they and similar early boats developed with higher engine power, they naturally grew in beam. Now the beam-length ratio is something more like 1 to 4 or 1 to 3.5. The chine lines are still low and flat, terminating in present-day boats at the outboard corners of a flat rectangular transom. The raked-transom type of deadrise boats are the older models which are also narrower in beam. They have a short overhanging

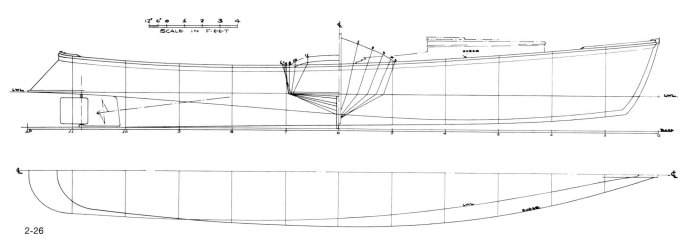

2-26

2-27

49

counter with a V transom. They were built when engine power was much lower and squatting was not a problem. They are undoubtedly more comfortable in a Chesapeake chop, and although they are no longer being built, many are still on the contemporary scene. These boats are periodically repowered with larger automobile engines and are thus forced to use "squat-boards," which effectively extend the waterline and prevent stern sinkage.

Generally the construction techniques of Chesapeake boats are similar and are motivated as much by simplicity as by tradition. There are some designers who will argue that V-bottom construction is as difficult and requires as much skill as round-bottom, steamed-frame construction. It is perhaps true that setting up the frame is comparable in the two methods, even granting the fact that the V-bottom or chine hull has five basic segments to a full frame plus its knees and gussets, while the round-bottom boat has only three. However, most Chesapeake chine boats, because of their sturdy cross-planked bottoms, find no need for bottom frames. The essential frames are heavy sawn timbers on the sides between chine and sheer clamp under the deck edge. While the bottom planking is set crosswise, often diagonally from the keel, the side is planked lengthwise in wide planks, about three to four strakes per side. In smaller craft as few as two or even one broad plank per side may be used. The comparative simplicity of planking in the Chesapeake manner is obviously more economical and adaptable in the Chesapeake, where the

fishermen are frequently their own builders, than the careful fitting, spiling, and beveling of the many planks used in round-bottom boats. This fact is most evident in the comparative cost of the two types of boats.

The deadrise hull form could stand some improvement. It would be highly desirable to lift the chine line well above the forward waterline and rake the stem forward, which would produce a flaring section and a finer waterline. The chine knuckle now present in Chesapeake craft would be virtually lost.

Only two elements — size and speed — can be considered similar when comparing the New England indigenous craft to those of the Chesapeake Bay.

Both are medium displacement hulls capable of length-speed ratios in the order of 2.0 at maximum power. Both types show strong local characteristics but, generally too, exhibit the individualities of their owners. Beyond this they are adapted to their own environments and employments as is proper.

In the Chesapeake boats, the individuality among oyster tongers may show in the location of the short, stubby mast: some are forward, some aft. In the small freight carriers and buy boats, the deckhouse is generally aft, but sometimes it is forward as is more prevalent in American boats elsewhere. There is frequently no shelter or cuddy in the smaller hand-tonging boats. This is no doubt so because their owners are the sons and grandsons of watermen who in earlier years sailed in small open crabbing skiffs and log canoes.

The most unique working boat in the Chesapeake is the oyster dredger. Because the law still
permits only very limited dredging of oysters by
powered vessels, the most distinctive of Chesapeake
craft works under sail. Old documents and regis-
trations officially referred to these boats as *bateaux,*
their generic name. Now these craft are popularly
known as *skipjacks*. The profile of a Chesapeake
skipjack is shown in Figure 2-30.

Dredging for oysters by sail power is motivated
by man-made laws for natural conservation, true,
but also natural law and efficient practice support
the use of sailing craft. It is a fact that an oyster
boat, moved by sail, will haul a dredge over an
oyster bed more gently and less destructively than
will a powered dredge boat. The oysters gathered
in this way may not taste better, but their shells
will be less damaged and they will go to market
fresh and "live." In addition, because the sailing
craft cannot clean off an oyster bar so efficiently as
can a powered craft, the crop will be conserved for
the future.

In recent years, the conservation laws have been
relaxed to allow two days per week when dredging
can be assisted by the engine power of the "yawl"
boats carried by each skipjack for pushing when the
skipjack is not employed in dredging. This change
in the rules is the result of an oyster blight and
allows the oyster dredgers to receive a more steady
profit from their most rugged work. There is
hardly any question that these sailing boats of the
Chesapeake would not exist without the protection
of state law. This artificial safeguard does, however, account for the existence of a working fleet of
sailing craft in a densely populated and highly in-
dustrialized region. The effectiveness of this type
of preservation, coupled with the conservation of
natural resources, could be a case for study. It has
many facets to recommend it.

Not too long ago, there were other types of sailing craft in the oyster fleet, such as the finely
modeled, round-bottom, two-masted bugeye, and
the round-bottom, gaff-headed oyster sloop. The
skipjack has survived longer because it essentially
has a shoal V-bottom form of heavy but more economical construction. She is comparatively simple
to build and operate. The dredging operation, as
may be seen in Figures 2-29 and 2-31, is essentially
the towing of a triangular steel frame with teeth
on the bottom and a heavy-net pocket over the
oyster bed at four to five knots. This speed must
be maintained because a faster speed would merely
bounce the dredge along over the high spots of the
bottom ineffectively, and a lower speed is less
efficient in filling the dredge. Consequently, both
jib and mainsail have three or four rows of reef-
points, and most winter dredging is done with sails
deeply reefed to keep the dredgeboat from going
too fast.

The average skipjack is approximately 45 to 50
feet long with a beam of 16 or more feet. She has
a shallow draft and carries a heavy centerboard.
She has a heavy, raked mast and the mainsail is
hooped to it, except for the upper portion between
the headstay and jibstay. The jib is on a partial
club and is self tending. She has a substantial bow-

2-29

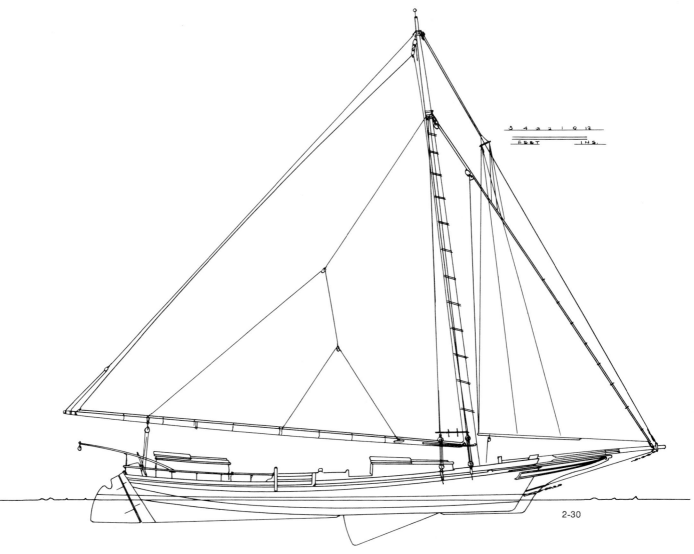

2-30

2-29   *A reefed oyster dredger working the beds.*

2-30   *The lines profile of a Chesapeake oyster dredger. Commonly referred to as a skipjack, this workboat is the last survivor of working sail in the waters of continental United States.*

2-31   *Two skipjacks dredging in the Bay.*

2-31

sprit above her clipper-type long head set on a raked stem. All these boats, like their predecessors, the bugeyes, pungys, and earlier Baltimore clipper schooners, carry highly decorated, painted, and carved headboards and trail knees at the bow.

The bow form of today's skipjack is truly American in origin. It first found favor in the Chesapeake on the fast Baltimore clippers. In the early nineteenth century, it became a trademark on small, raked-mast schooners and brigs sailing in the revenue service and the merchant trade to the Caribbean, Mediterranean, and African coast. It was later used on the great Yankee clippers in a more restrained form and consequently is still popularly referred to as a clipper bow. A similar bow form can be found on some small craft in the Mediterranean today, but it is of a far older and different design. It is discussed further in Chapter 5.

Skipjacks are characteristically fitted with taffrails and have stern davits for their yawl boats. The rudder is hung outboard of the broad transom, but steering is through a linkage from the rudder head to a steering wheel. These boats in their rig, construction, and overall appearance reflect the essential and inherent ruggedness of working sailing craft, but they are unfortunately diminishing in number each year. At this writing there are only two score still working, and they are decreasing at the rate of five percent each year.

The skipjack is a unique American workboat. It is the only one under sail in continental United States, or, as a cohesive fleet, in the western hemisphere. As a sailing craft, its hull form is effective and practical, well adapted to its employment. It is stiff and able under sail; however, its flat, beamy hull of chine form leaves much to be desired when going to windward.

The skipjack, as a type, was developed only about 75 years ago as a more economical fishing craft than the sleeker, faster bugeye. The bugeye, with its two-masted ketch-type rig, is essentially a well-molded double-ender. She has a round-bottomed hull framed and planked in the manner of older and larger sailing vessels. The skipjack, with a V-bottom chine-form hull, is far more economical to build, and with her greater beam and flare of sides can carry more oysters. Skipjacks and bugeyes existed together for more than 50 years, but as replacements were made the owners naturally chose the skipjack. As a consequence there are today no bugeyes in use.

The bugeye developed sometime after the Civil War to satisfy a growing demand for oysters. This demand, which from the early nineteenth Century was quite brisk, had been responsible for the exploitation of newly found oyster beds in the Chesapeake by smaller craft of the Chesapeake log-canoe type. The log canoes grew into the larger and similarly rigged brogans of approximately 25 to 30 feet. The brogan was actually a small bugeye. Both bugeyes and brogans were the most efficient working craft under sail, but as commercial boats they inevitably lost the race with economy of construction and engine-powered propulsion. The skipjack today is the most economical survivor of the Chesapeake sailing workboats.

2-33

2-32 A Chesapeake log canoe at the annual Oxford regatta. Note the two hiking boards to windward.

2-33 Beach repairs in the Bahamas. This out-island has a hetrogeneous assortment of working sloops. The hull in the left foreground exhibits a typical underbody with some drag.

There is but one other purely indigenous sailing workboat type in North American waters. In the Bahama Islands a distinctive, flourishing, and indigenous fleet of *sloops* and *catboats* still exists.

The Bahama sloop, like other sailing workboats, survives marginally. But there is in this environment an ideal combination of elements accounting for the natural survival of the sailing fleet. There is first the strong trade wind that blows consistently and reliably. Also the waters are protected from the ocean by the natural ring of islands and the shallow Bahama banks. The islands are well off the paths of commerce, and their resources will support only a relatively small population. The population centers on the various islands are within comfortable sailing distances of each other.

Transportation is ideally by boat and preferably the leisurely sort provided by sail. The employment of the boats is in both fishing and light cargo transport. The fishing is confined most profitably to gathering conches, and catching fish like groupers, and when these items are ready for market, they are generally transported to Nassau.

These sloops and catboats exist in an economic never-never land. They are a special case for survival, as are any sailing workboats still surviving. Here in the out-islands, the true islanders are genuinely poor or else money is of far less importance to their graceful way of life. Surrounded by rich, seasonal, off-island tourists and winter guests, whose money is also of little consequence to them, these boats continue to provision and supply transport. The Bahamas sloops are a classic example of the parallel existence of a marginal economy and a commercially successful one.

Bahamian skippers, like all good seamen, pay good attention to the maintenance of their boats. They are generally painted three times a year and are provided a new set of cotton sails every third year. The annual competition of the Out Island Regatta serves additionally to generate pride and maintenance in these fine boats.

The Bahama sloops, like the now-obsolete Bermuda sloops, are descendants of the eighteenth century English sloops and cutters. They still retain much of this original character in their configuration. The boats vary in size from 20 to as much as 40 feet in length. A typical lines form is shown in Figure 2-34. Construction is solid: heavy planks on sawn frames cut from native Caribbean mahogany-like wood, known as "horseflesh." The frames are often made from natural crooks. The hull is deep-heeled with a characteristic broad wine-glass transom on which is hung an outboard rudder. The stem is usually straight and unadorned, but often is seen with a bowsprit over a clipper-profile stem knee.

It is worth emphasizing that the type of sail on the Bahama sloop is most distinctive. Without much doubt, it is the living prototype of the earliest north European fore-and-aft sail. At the turn of the century, the western world's sailing yachts carried the universally used gaff-rigged mainsails, generally with tall gaff topsails on additional spars above. Thus a large gaff-rigged racing sloop with

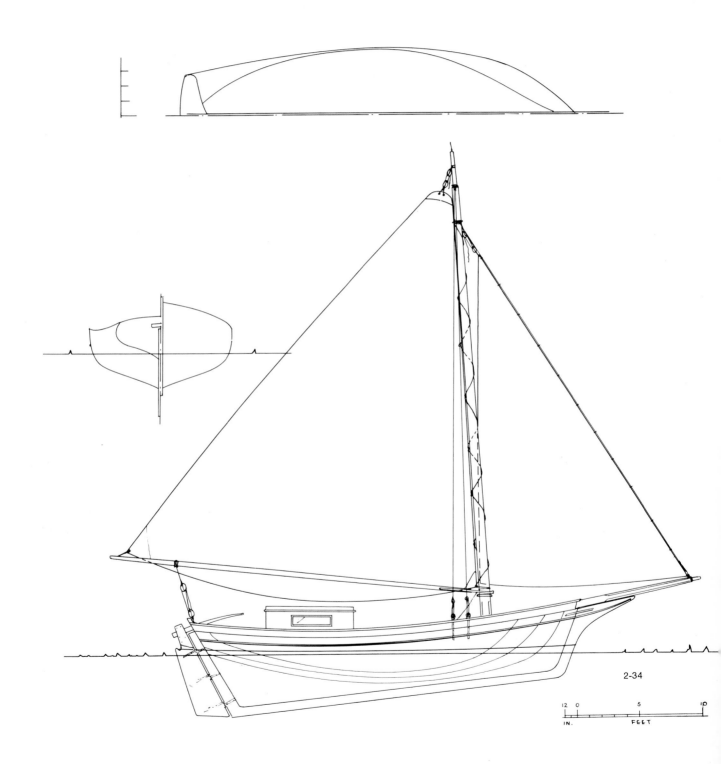

2-34

2-34   *The lines and profile of a Bahama sloop with a characteristic clipper stem form. Many of today's sloops have straight stems and no bowsprit. These craft are generally larger than and are related to the sharp-shooter model, which carried only a mainsail on a mast stepped well forward.*

2-35   *Two sloops of the Bahamas in their best dress for the annual workboats regatta of the Out-Islands. Note the small club topsail, a clever use of a main topsail with a jib-headed mainsail — a fairly common practice in the Bahamas.*

her heavy gaff and a topsail on the top-mast with two long clubs at its luff and foot had a very complex and top-heavy rig. There is little wonder that the simple triangular sail set on a single but taller mast was gradually almost universally accepted after its introduction. Because of its similarity in shape to the sails of the Bermuda and Bahama sloops, it was often called the Bermudian rig and is so referred to still in England. Actually, the Bermudian rig, or, as referred to more frequently in the United States, the jib-headed or Marconi rig, is similar *only* in the shape of its sail to that of a Bahama sloop and very approximately so at that. The Bahama sail is nearly as long on the boom as it is on the mast. It is loose-footed and fills with a very large draft, which gives it a baggy shape. The cloths of the sail are sewn parallel to the leech instead of "cross cut" as are more conventional modern sails. The sail has a large headboard or (preferably) a miniature gaff hoisted on a single halyard. This gaff is undoubtedly the surviving element of the original Dutch hooked gaff introduced in the early seventeenth century and adopted shortly after by the British in their American colonies.

South of the Bahamas in the Caribbean, the working boats almost defy clear indigenous classification. There are some exceptions, of course, such as the Belizean sloops, the Trinidad pirogues, the Martinique pirogues, the St. Kitts sailing lighters, and perhaps a characteristic trading sloop. However, the more important and overriding distinction of these vessels is what may be called their "Caribbean character."

The small, indigenous working boats of the Caribbean are still largely sailing craft, most frequently of the poorest and least adequately equipped sort. Their designs and rigs reflect the same ancestry as the boats of the Bahamas. They are not, however, as well preserved. They are most generally built by their owners on the banks of rivers or in the less active corners of small ports near the sources of an indifferent selection of boat-building timber. The hulls are old and patched even when they are first launched; their masts and spars are often selected from available trees with

2-35

2-36   The hull lines of a typical Belizean
sloop of Honduras show a nicely modeled,
low-freeboard hull. The sails are typical
Caribbean sails except for the balanced jib
with its club pivoted on the stem head.

2-37   The lines of a Trinidad pirogue built
with a dugout log in place of the keel. The
rest of the hull is basically clinker-built.

only the bark removed. These characteristics, as well as their basic inherited, good form, identify them as indigenously Caribbean.

Some Caribbean craft do stand up better than others, reflecting a little better economic life or consistant maintenance by their owners. Among these are the sloops of Belize in Honduras. These boats are 22 to 30 feet long with sturdy cedar-planked hulls on natural crook frames of Santa Maria (a type of wood similar to oak). The lines of a typical Belizean sloop are shown in Figure 2-36. While it is similar to the Bahama type, it is essentially shallower. The rig is also similar, except there is a stemhead balanced jib boom instead of a bowsprit. The boats are steered with a kind of yoke on the rudder head in place of a tiller. (This yoke is taken along by the skipper whenever he leaves his boat.)   The sloops are used for fishing, primarily, and some have live fish or bait wells cut and boxed into their bottom. When so fitted they are called "smacks" instead of sloops. There are perhaps 30 of these boats that continue to work in the waters off Honduras.

In the Virgin Islands there was until recently a kind of sailing workboat that was known as a St. Kitts or Nevis sailing lighter. These heavy, sloop-rigged craft had very full and deep-bodied hulls and were simply a larger, fuller version of the average inter-island sloop, designed for cargo capacity consistent with their employment. They measured about 50 feet in length and nearly 20 feet in beam.

In the eastern Caribbean, in the area from Trinidad up through the Grenadines, the character of the boats shows a much greater variation. The boats reflect, more than other Caribbean boats, continental European influences rather than British. This is especially true of a small open boat, now powered, in Trinidad, called simply a pirogue. Figure 2-37 shows the lines of one of these boats together with a section showing the typical structure. The boats vary between 20 and 24 feet in length and are often powered by outboard engines or low-horsepower inboard engines. They generally are fitted with a live fish well amidships. The construction of these craft is most interesting and relates closely to that of very early primitive craft. While they are essentially of lapstrake construction, the backbone is a hollowed log. This construction represents an evolutionary stage in boat development of primitive communities. It was first used by the ancient Egyptians (see Chapter 1) when they first built planked-up hulls. It was also a stage in the development of Norse boats after they abandoned the more primitive frame and skin craft and built their early versions of lapstrake-planked hulls. It is a most logical process here because primitive log dugout boats have been used in the Caribbean for many centuries — no one knows exactly how long.

Pirogues are also still in use among the Antilles. They are particularly in evidence on Martinique, where there are most colorful, trim-lined, beach pirogues. These boats have a high freeboard with fine ends, and an unusual, extended, sharp, blade-like bow skeg. The boats have as many as six to eight pairs of crooked knee-like frames to reinforce the sides and support the upper plank, which pro-

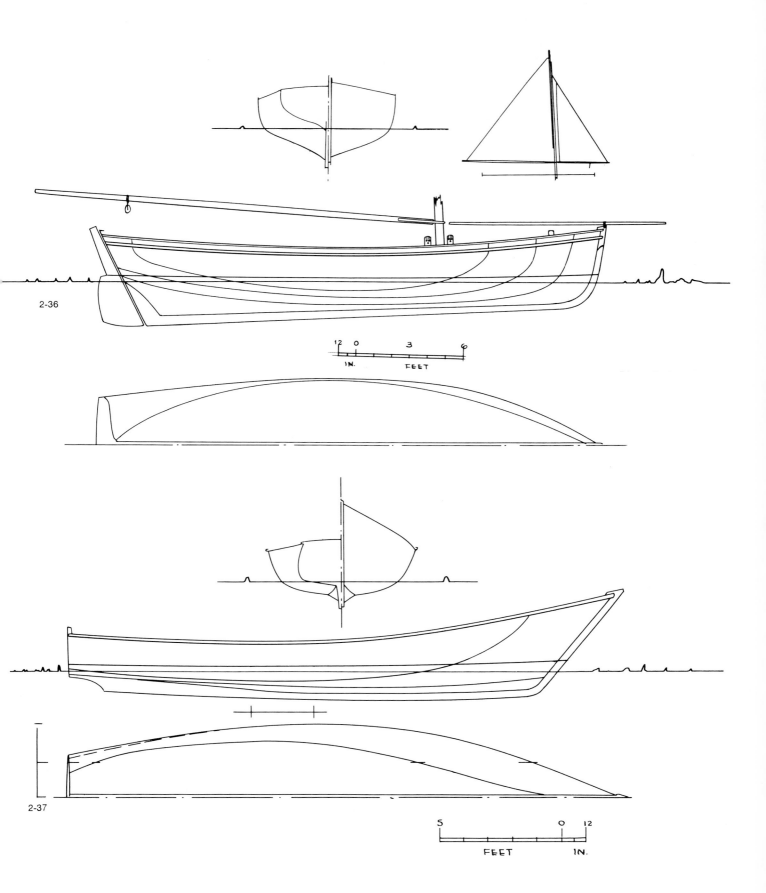

2-36

```
'12  0        3          6
  IN.        FEET
```

2-37

```
5                    0    12
        FEET              IN.
```

2-38 A St. Lucia canoe drawn up on shore presenting a clear view of her unusual extended blade-like bow.

2-39 A St. Lucia canoe under a native sprit-sail rig. Her extended bow is just visible below the painted waterline.

2-40 The profile of an Antilles fishing sloop. This boat, which was observed in Antigua, is well built of good materials, a practice that is not too common in the Caribbean.

2-41 The hull lines of a typical, but not standard, Antilles fishing sloop.

2-39

vides the necessary depth to the hull. These boats, together with the pirogues of Trinidad, are prime examples of true indigenous Carib craft, exhibiting, as they do, successive states of basic development.

Among the indigenous boat types of the world, there are a greater number of dugout-log craft than any other type of more sophisticated construction. There are more dugouts, also, that could be noted in the Caribbean region, and on the rivers of Central America, especially in Honduras. Also, others proliferate in South America, Africa, and many other regions of the world where there are people living in primitive or near aboriginal environments. To avoid repetition, I have made no attempt to describe all of them. In Chapter 1, however, where the structural development of boats is reviewed, the West African dugout-log fishing craft was selected as an existing prototype of all dugout boats.

The Caribbean sloop is most representative of the better small sailing craft of the area. It is a boat that has been described as a poor relative of the Bahama craft. Such an observation might seem unfair, but because of the proximity of these regions, comparisons are inevitable. As the typical Caribbean sloop, one could do no better than to choose a boat frequently associated with the Leeward Islands of the Lesser Antilles. The hull lines and sail plan in Figures 2-40 and 2-41 illustrate a typical sloop of Antigua, which is 25 feet long, 8 feet in beam, and 4 feet in draft. Such boats are well built in St. Johns, Antigua, on plain but clean

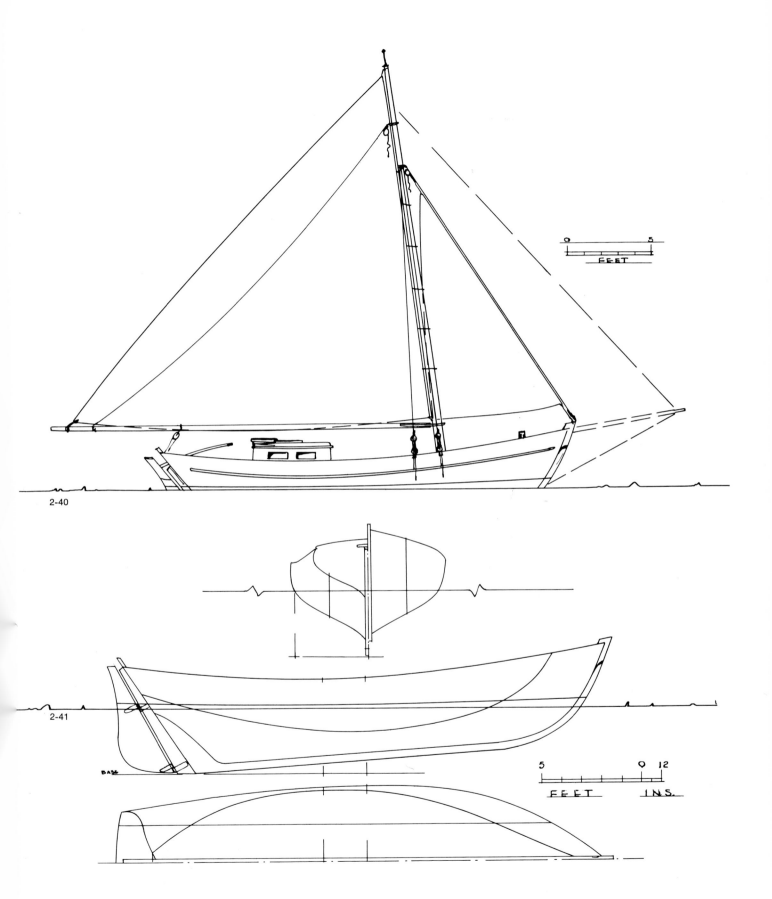

2-40

2-41

BASE

0   5
FEET

5   0   12
FEET   INS.

2-42 *A large working sloop of the Grenadines with double headsails. A boat of this size and in such good condition is seldom found outside the Antilles and the south-eastern portion of the Caribbean.*

2-43 *The Gulf Coast shrimp boat shows its relationship to the old Greek spongers in its lively sheer line and full bow. The boat itself is a purely American development, and modern shrimpers with this basic configuration are built in lengths over 80 feet and are used in many fisheries of the Western Hemisphere.*

2-42

sailing lines showing a deep-heeled hull, broad transom stern, and low cutter-sloop rig. The rake of the transom and curve of the stempost may be slightly greater than the Bermuda model; otherwise the similarity is close. The hull structure is framed in the same way from the same type of local woods, while the planking is pitch pine and must be imported. The builders, like most true indigenous boatbuilders, work by eye, experience, and simple rules. For example, the depth of the hull is half of the extreme beam measured about one-third of the length from forward; the depth is taken from the deck edge to the top of the keel vertically. The rig is also constructed by rule of thumb, with both the boom and the mast height from deck to truck being the overall length on deck of the hull. These traditions after several generations have become almost superstitions and in many cases are inviolable. A recent effort has been made to teach the builders (who are in some respects receptive to ideas to improve their means and ways) how to build with steam-bent rather than sawn frames. Such a technique would allow faster construction and lighter, stronger hulls with more internal room. Unfortunately, this requires that builders be able to read plans in order to lay out the molds (see Chapter 1). Many of the builders in this area have expressed the need for further help in training courses for shipwrights.

Regardless of their age and condition, which in some Caribbean regions is deplorable, Caribbean boats still provide needed lifelines among the native island population. They will for a long time

2-43

to come. These boats, under sail, are impressive and handsome. Figure 2-42 shows an Antilles sloop moving out from an island in the Grenadines — a typical Caribbean sloop in a typical Caribbean setting.

One constant factor in the character of boats engaged in shrimp catching in the various regions of the world is their greatly varied designs. The designs vary largely because of the different techniques of harvesting the shellfish. In England there are still some shrimp boats or "prawners" working under sail as small sloop-rigged boats. In Portugal the heavy little shrimp trawlers are operated from the beaches. But in the United States, where shrimping is one of the more profitable fisheries, the shrimp trawler has evolved in the last 50 years to become a most formidable boat. Originally developed in Florida, this indigenous design has spread throughout the Gulf Coast region even as far as Mexico, and the type can be identified in use along the east coast of South America.

The shrimper began as a variation of an improved powerboat based on the Greek sponge boat of the west coast of Florida. But unlike the sponge boat, which cannot be identified as an indigenous American craft because of its close identity to the Greek spongers of the Aegean, the Gulf shrimp trawler has become a true American boat indigenous to the southern coast. After a relatively quick development period, it reached its present characteristic form and style about 40 years ago, though it was then a relatively small boat of 30 to 50 feet in length. This shrimper style is reminiscent of the old Greek boats in its full-bodied hull, sweeping sheer line, and fine entrance. It is otherwise purely a powerboat hull. It was perhaps the first type of powered fishing craft of any size to have the pilot-house located forward. This is possibly because the early boats had no power winches and the trawl was hauled by hand. The crew wanted a maximum of free working deck area aft. Thus when most European and American trawlers were locating their deckhouses aft, these shrimp trawlers with forward deckhouses were unusual. The design has remained largely unchanged, and the present-day Gulf coast shrimpboat continues to grow both in number and size. The lines form of a typical shrimper appears in Figure 2-44. The most popular size is about 65 feet in length, although larger boats of this type are built, often to supply other fishing industries.

The typical shrimper is heavily built of the best domestic woods and materials. The stem is of choice Appalachian white oak; the keel is a single unscarfed piece of Douglas fir; the planking from keel to waterline is of cypress and from waterline to deck is of Douglas fir. The frames are of steam-bent white oak, and the decks and transom are of yellow pine. The fastenings are of heavily galvanized steel bolts and boat nails.

The shrimpboat of today, while larger and more handsomely equipped than that of 30 years ago, hauls lighter trawls and so is rigged with twin outrigger booms in a double-rigged trawl arrange-

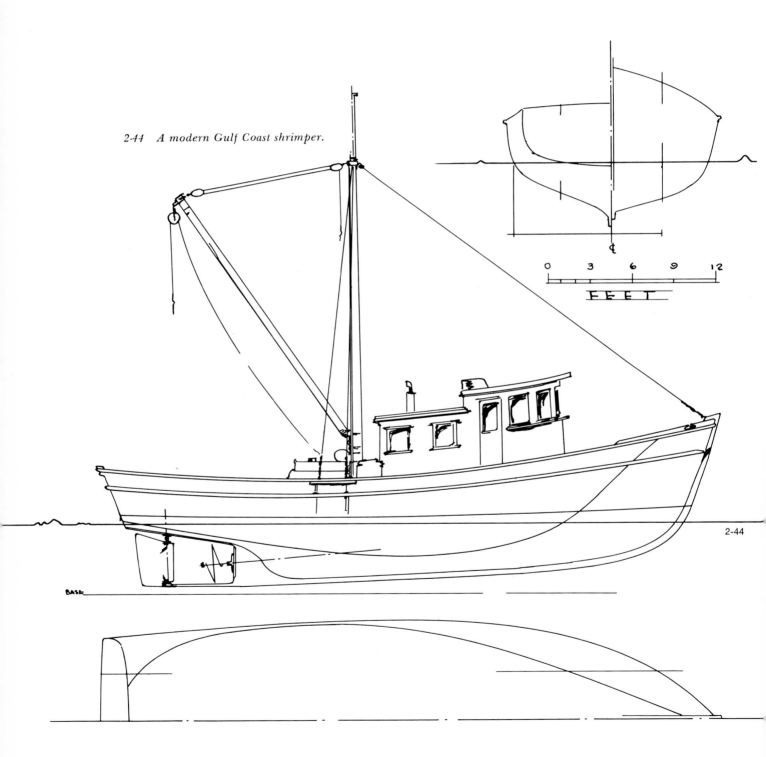

2-44   *A modern Gulf Coast shrimper.*

0   3   6   9   12

FEET

2-44

BASE

ment. The boat's form provides a dry foredeck. It is generally a good sea boat except for a rather excessive rolling tendency, caused, primarily, by its full, round sections.

Shrimpers are most rugged, capable boats, and I can personally attest to their resistance to underwater damage. In the late 1940's we took a trip up the Chesapeake in a small Florida shrimper. We had four sailing craft in tow and were making a good seven knots when we struck the unmarked submerged foundation of an old lighthouse. The impact threw us off our feet and ripped off the propeller after moving the shaft out of its coupling. The boat was firmly aground on hard, jagged concrete, resting on her keel and bilge, and the tide was running out. The boat remained there without taking on a significant amount of water until the next high tide, when she was taken in tow. The damage proved to be confined to the propeller and shaft, with only minor scuffing of the keel and bottom planking.

On the west coast of Mexico where the ancient Aztec culture flourished several hundred years before Columbus crossed the Atlantic, there is a type of fishing craft that is perhaps the last example of any truly native American boat. The natives of the American continents, both north and south, were never noted for their seagoing inclinations. Aside from the large war canoes of some North American tribes that were used almost exclusively on rivers and lakes, there is no evidence of any water-

craft of open-water ability before the arrival of the Europeans.

On the Pacific shores of Mexico, there are some dugout-log boats of interesting and sophisticated character undoubtedly related to the pre-Columbian cultures of this land. These boats today are abundant in the coastal regions beyond the Sierra Madre del Sur range. The hulls are adzed from single large logs of parota wood and may be as long as 28 to 30 feet, with a beam of four feet, or slightly more. Their shapes vary slightly, but there is a consistency of form that distinguishes these boats from the log canoes of river, jungle, and most tropical island regions. These boats are shaped with a graceful sheer curve that obviously adapts them to ocean beaches and surf launching. It is this characteristic more than any other that separates canoes from boats. The bow and stern forms of these Mexican boats also exhibit a utilitarian rake, which combined with the sheer line, produces an overall pleasing functional sea-boat shape. Figures 2-45 and 2-46 show fair examples of these boats along the Acapulco beaches. Like all dugout-log boats they must be protected from drying and cracking. A little water is always left in the bilges, and the boats are covered when hauled out with wetted canvas or, in the older manner, with palm fronds. As most dugouts, these boats have long lives — generally more than 50 years and sometimes a century — and they are closely linked with the past. That these Mexican dugouts originated from the old Aztec culture is apparent in the reserved decorations and painting patterns on the hulls. These continu-

65

2-45

2-46

through a crest of surf, and painted with a bright edging border below the sheer with half a dozen of the brightest colors. Today these boats work within sight of the glittering luxury hotels of Acapulco.

The working craft of the Pacific coast of North America are nowadays highly systematized, mostly owned and operated by large and wealthy companies. The tuna-fishing industry now operates highly engineered and professionally designed vessels whose individual costs may exceed two and a half million dollars. These conditions are similar in the shrimping industry of the Atlantic and Gulf coast. The systems approach is perhaps the most efficient way to supply the market demands for popular seafood products, but it has largely eliminated small owner-operated indigenous boats.

There is still to be found on the Pacific coast, however, a type of boat that has developed strong indigenous character during the twentieth century. These boats are found most frequently along the central California coast, but many may work farther north or south. They are known generally as the "Monterey boats." Their basic identifying features are a beamy round-bottom hull, a full double-ended form, and a type of clipper bow of Mediterranean origin. The bow form is generously flared and the stern is extended in a characteristic curving rake, giving the whole hull a pleasing and graceful line. Some more modern versions have a full, round stern eliminating the older double-ended form. Some still carry double rub wales along the side with vertical stiffeners which make a very

ous abstract patterns encircling the hulls from end to end are the same patterns and styles used in the pictograms painted by the Mixtec people who lived in the Oaxaca valley about 1000 A.D. It is most likely that the Mixtecs fished from boats very much like today's — adzed out of parota wood, shaped with a graceful sheer and good freeboard to rise

2-45 Side view of an Acapulco dugout. Note the outboard bracket at the stern.

2-46 Bow view of an Acapulco dugout. The nets hung to dry are used for seining sardines along the beach.

heavy and strong side structure reminiscent of the early fourteenth and fifteenth century caravel construction. These boats are heavily framed, sometimes with the older type of sawn frames or, in recent boats, with heavy steamed frames. The entire form and structure strongly suggest a Latin European influence. This likeness is in no way the result of a direct copy of any Mediterranean craft, as were the earlier San Francisco feluccas. It is, rather, the result of second or third generation traditional influences which have resulted in a healthy and thoroughly sea-capable form which embodies much Old World character. These Monterey boats of today can only be thought of as truly American types because they have no predecessors and have grown to suit their American environment and employment.

Monterey boats, as their name implies, are found in and around Monterey, California, and the San Francisco area. The simplified profile and plan of a typical Monterey boat are shown in Figure 2-47, and the individual variations in structure and details can readily be seen in Figure 2-48.

The dimensions of Monterey boats are represented by one example measuring 42 feet length, 12 feet beam, and 4½ feet draft. They are generally of about 12 to 13 tons full displacement and are frequently employed and rigged as trollers. As such, their tall outrigger poles give them a most rakish appearance.

A more modern, but still distinctive, boat type known as the Pacific "combination" fishing boat is engaged in the same independent employment in the West Coast fisheries as the Monterey boat. This type is characterized by trollers and purse seiners of similar and repetitious form, and can be found along much of the West Coast. The characteristics of the combination boat have not been entirely the result of the natural selective processes that normally produce other indigenous boats — professional designers have entered into the picture. This type, nevertheless, seems to be preferred by discriminating fishermen and is thus laying a strong claim to being a native American boat. This particular type has also acquired considerable popularity on the Pacific coast of South America.

There are many much larger combination boats, but Figure 2-51 shows the profile of a typical troller of this design. This example is of a relatively small boat 36 feet long, 10½ feet beam, and 4 feet draft that has adopted the double-ended stern with the curved stern post used on Monterey boats and the Maine sardine carrier, a feature common in European boats. This, in conventional naval architectural terms, is normally called a canoe stern, but on fishing craft instead of yachts and larger vessels it seems more natural and less contrived. It is, thus, generally recognized as a *trawler* stern. (See Figure 2-50.)

The more common variation of this typical Pacific coast combination fishing boat may be seen in Figure 2-52. This example is 42½ feet long, 12 feet in beam, 5 feet in draft, and rigged as a seiner. The heavy construction and typical rounded-square tugboat-type stern is evident in this longitudinal section. This is a most practical and common stern

2-47   The hull configuration of a typical Monterey boat. The original Mediterranean character and heritage is apparent in these basic lines.

2-48   Monterey boats along Fishermen's Wharf, San Francisco. Note the Old World-style rub rails on the boat in the foreground.

2-49   A small West Coast dragger.

2-50   A double-ended combination boat from Port Angeles. This is a rugged seagoing fishing boat indigenous to the north Pacific coast of the United States.

2-51   The hull form of a small double-ended combination boat. This boat is most typical of the Puget Sound area.

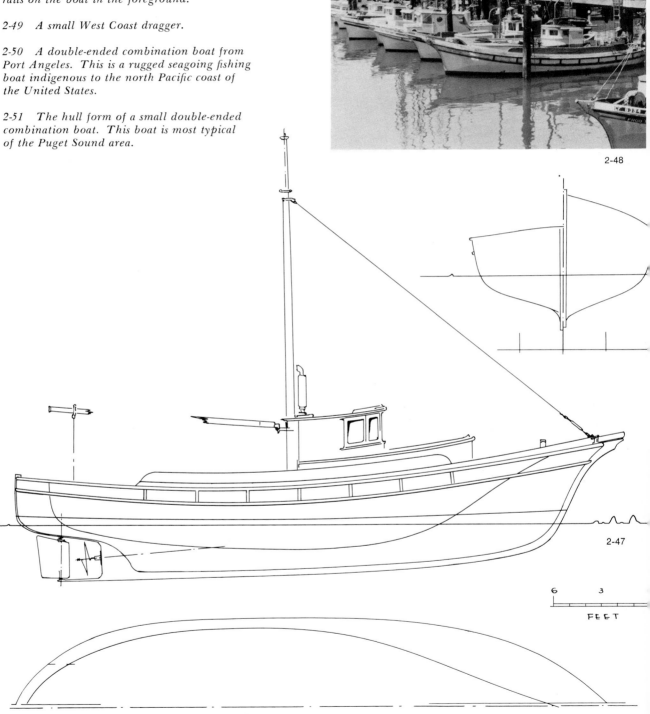

2-48

2-47

6   3

FEET

2-49

2-50

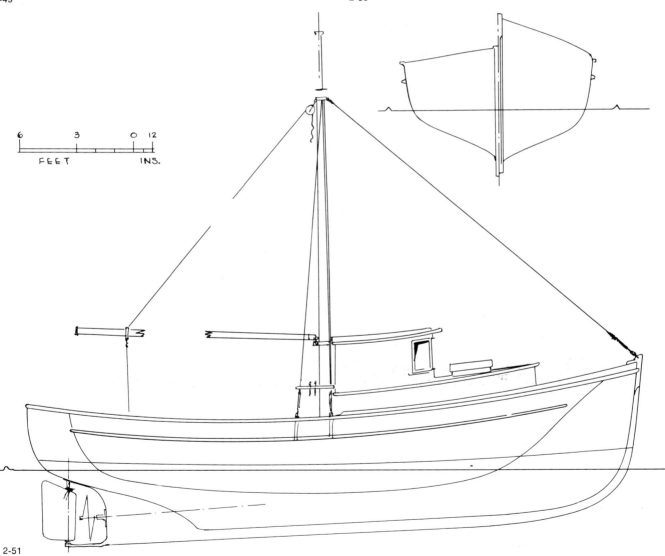

2-51

2-52   The profile of an old but serviceable combination boat of the northern California and Oregon coast. These boats engage in the sardine industry and are often rigged as seiners, but, as the name combination implies, they are easily adapted to other techniques of other fisheries.

2-53   A combination boat of the California coast typical of the hull configuration shown in Figure 2-52. This is a hard-working, well-kept, privately owned fishing boat.

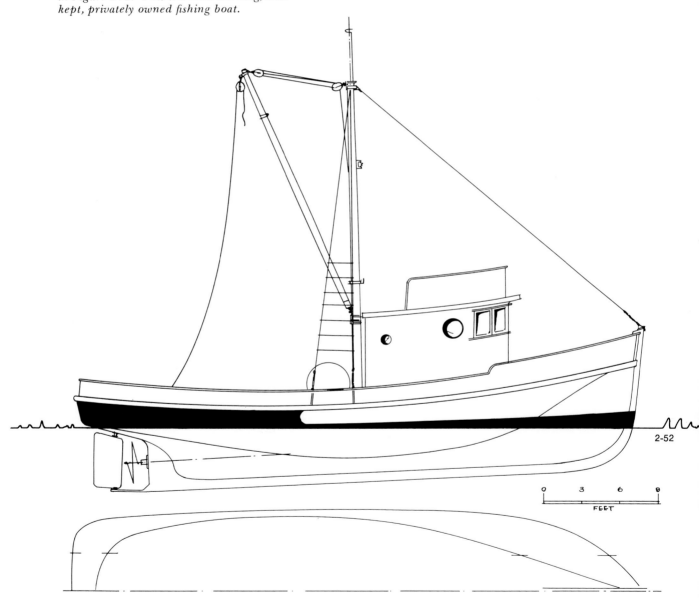

2-52

0   3   6   9

FEET

2-53

used on West Coast boats that provides a broad and stable working platform. Figure 2-53 shows a boat of this type, but slightly larger with a slight variation in her deck profile and rail height.

In recent years welded steel construction has become increasingly popular. With welding skills and techniques improving, it is quite probable that many more boats will be built this way. The external appearance of a steel boat is very little different from that of a wooden boat.

I have been deliberately selective in describing American boats. Only healthy functional types of working boats that exhibit strong regional characteristics have been discussed. It is interesting in retrospect to remark on the influence that several of these have had on the development of more universal boat designs. The character and style of the majority of the better pleasure craft have their origins in these regional types of working boats. The most outstanding examples of this can be seen on the east and west coasts of the United States.

The New England lobsterboats and the more beamy lapstrake New Jersey sea skiffs have contributed much to the configurations and styles of the most successful sport-fishing boats as well as many power cruisers, pilot boats, and commercially designed tenders.

The V-bottom construction of the Chesapeake Bay craft has contributed heavily to the design of the smaller, more economical pleasure cruiser. V-section hull forms with their simplified construction and more easily molded shapes were not used before the introduction of mechanical propulsion. With increased speed and power demands this characteristic shape became the base from which to develop the more efficient chine hull with cleaner entrances, flatter runs, and broader sterns. Such hull forms provide optimum utilization of interior space. While they may reach high-speed planing operation more easily in protected water, they do not distinguish themselves in more rugged sea conditions as well as do the modified round-bottom hulls mentioned previously.

The larger, heavier fishing craft of the Pacific coast, such as the trollers, seiners, and combination boats, have set a pattern for a healthy and popular type of yacht misnamed a "trawler" yacht. This sort of cruising yacht is being built in increasing numbers and represents a desirable trend away from the high sided, glassed-in, over-powered stock design cruisers of recent years.

The tendency of naval architects, competent yacht designers, and discriminating builders and buyers to observe, refine, and promote the features of healthy working boats is most reassuring. This is not to infer or recommend that replicas and facsimiles for pleasure use are the ultimate or even desirable goal. Direct conversions from working craft to pleasure craft are seldom successful. However the recognition and employment of the basic features of sea kindliness, simplicity, and performance where they are applicable are substantive evidence of the worth of native American working boats.

3 / NORTHERN EUROPEAN WORKING CRAFT

Northern Europe has produced some of the most capable, small, indigenous working boats in all the world. Some of these boats have been models of excellence to be copied in other lands. At the same time some have remained unique because craftsmen from other lands have neither understood them nor adapted tempermentally to duplicate them. A combination of factors, such as a heavy weather environment, sturdy native woods, and disciplined craftsmen have contributed to all of the native boats of northern Europe. These boats sail in the semi-protected but rugged waters of the Baltic, in the arctic waters off the Norwegian coast, and in the Skagerrak and Kattegat. They are found in remote harbors in the fjords of Norway, the Danish Islands, the lowlands of Holland, the Hebrides, the Orkneys, the Channel coast, and other ports or coves between. This is a most extensive environment, yet there is a common bond of purpose and cultural influence that produces a similarity of structure in all northern European boats. Since this is not a complete encyclopedia of boats nor catalog of geographical types, I will not follow the principle that *all* examples both good and mediocre, however remote, must be located and described. Instead, the best, and, sometimes, the most interesting will be discussed.

It is best to look at the Netherlands first, because of its central geographical location, and because its extensive maritime tradition and centuries-old determination to wrest land and living from the sea has produced a rich variety of unique boats.

Along the coast of Holland, there is much land lying below the level of the sea. This land is constantly being reclaimed from the sea and maintained by the Dutch, who must rely on watercraft adapted to shallow water and restricted channels. So these craft are not only indigenous, but they are also ingeniously unique.

Because of the lowland nature of Holland, with its network of canals and open, shallow waters, the most characteristic feature of Dutch watercraft is their shoal draft. Upon first view these boats all seem to be molded on bluff, full lines, almost barge-like. In a sense they are, but after fuller examination and study, one realizes their configurations, all basically similar, are of a more subtle and complex character. The orientation of their entrances as well as their runs is rotated ninety degrees from customary form. The bows are excessively full above the waterline, with a maximum beam noticeably forward of amidships. The form leads into a shallow bottom with flat buttocks, a shape essentially designed to allow a maximum of flow under the hull. These hulls, when underway, either under power or sail at maximum speed, do not cause a very deep bow wave. Disturbance of the water is relatively slight, amounting primarily to splashing, broken water at the stem and other forward surfaces. There is no cleavage of the water; it is not forced away from the stem or forefoot as in most hulls with vertical, sharp stems and fine waterline entrances. Hence the wave pattern is largely muted and progress through the water is most economical. These are general features, typical of the various shallow-draft inshore craft, which are es-

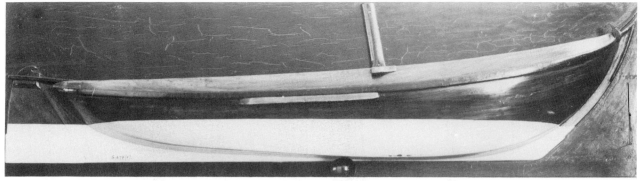

sentially the indigenous ones. The varied construction features of these boats produce types that differ from region to region and with the nature of their employment.

There are three or four basic types of smaller Dutch workboats, up to approximately 50 feet in length. These are; the *botter,* the *hoogaars,* the *boeier,* and the *schokker.* A larger but similar craft is called the *tjalk.* These craft are shown in Figures 3-1, 3-2, 3-3, and 3-4.

At times, these characteristic Dutch craft seem contrived when viewed against a backdrop of windmills and wooden shoes. There is no doubt that the people of Holland know how unique these boats are and, perhaps with official approval and assistance, maintain them as an attractive link with a nineteenth century Holland — the same Holland tourists want to see.

These traditional boats of Holland deserve description, however, because they contain the origins of whatever indigenous qualities still lurk in Dutch boats of today. The motor barges, produce boats, and small freight boats largely evolved from the characteristic shapes of the traditional craft. The indigenous hulls, where they exist, are most frequently converted tjalks of 50 to 70 feet, built of steel. They are still working under power carrying produce and commerce. Some sailing workboats have become yachts and still have their rigs preserved.

The *boeier* is the most shapely and graceful of the traditional craft. It is also perhaps the generic one, in that it is the model that the seventeenth and eighteenth century Dutch yachts were built on. It is characterized by its lapstrake planking, rounded sections with noticeable deadrise, distinctive tumblehome in the sheer plank, and upswept ends. Often the bottom planks are carvel and laid parallel to the keel for most of the length. The fullest beam is forward of amidships.

The *botter* is similar to the *boeier.* The most distinctive difference between the two is the flat bottom of the botter and its carvel planking throughout. The stem on both the boeier and the botter is gracefully rounded in profile, generally terminating with a sharply defined crescent-shaped end. The characteristic, modern rig of these boats is called a bezan. It essentially consists of a loose-footed gaff-rigged mainsail with a short, hooked gaff; an overlapping staysail; and in light weather a jib from a bowsprit rigged on the starboard side of the stem.

The *boeiers* and the *botters* today have mostly been converted to yachts and private craft, sailing for pleasure on the Ijssel Meer (formerly the Zuider Zee) or providing pleasant houseboat accommodations in a quiet canal. They vary from 30 to 50 feet in length. The original construction was of the heaviest sort of sawn frame with thick planking (either lap or carvel as indicated).

When the boeiers and botters were working boats for either freight transport or fishing, they had a large hold in the full hulls that could be almost completely uncovered by a system of removable hatch covers. A graceful house with a pronounced crown as well as sheer was located well

3-1   The form of the botter is uniquely Dutch. This half model shows the flat bottom of a botter in contrast to its complex, curved hull.

3-2   The hoogaars has a simple, rugged hull with flat sections and a flat bottom. It was originally the poor man's workboat and was indigenous to the region of Flushing and the island of Walcheren, Holland.

3-3   The boeier has a full, round bottom. Undoubtedly it is the oldest Dutch boat form, and quite likely it is the most basic of all Dutch boats.

3-4   The schokker is similar in basic form to the hoogaars but is generally larger and smooth planked. This type is frequently found in western Holland in the Scheldt estuary region.

3-2

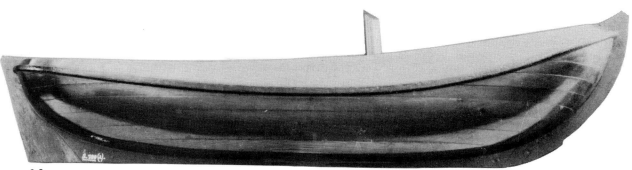

3-3

3-4

3-5　The sail plan of a boeier is similar to that of the botter. This example shows the lower rig of a working boat. This unique bezan-type sail plan has a characteristic pleasing proportion and, when seen on the waters of the Ijjsel Meer, has a grace and simplicity typical only of Holland.

3-6　A botter that has been converted to a pleasure craft. These boats are comfortable and cruise capably in semi-sheltered waters. Their popularity is evident in their frequent appearance in Mediterranean and British ports, and sometimes on the Chesapeake Bay.

3-7　The lines of a botter show her characteristic fullness over the flat bottom. This boat, with her full bow, tends to ride high and create less of a bow wave system than would be expected.

3-8　The sail plan of the botter in this example is somewhat loftier than generally seen on working boats. The stays are rigged on running tackles for lowering the rig frequently.

3-6

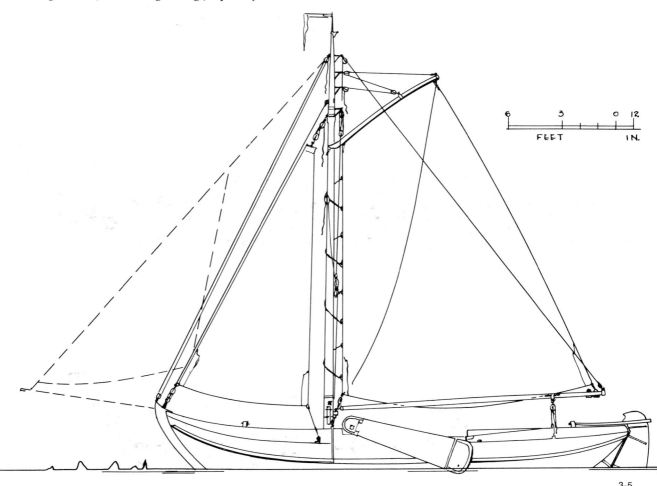

3-5

76

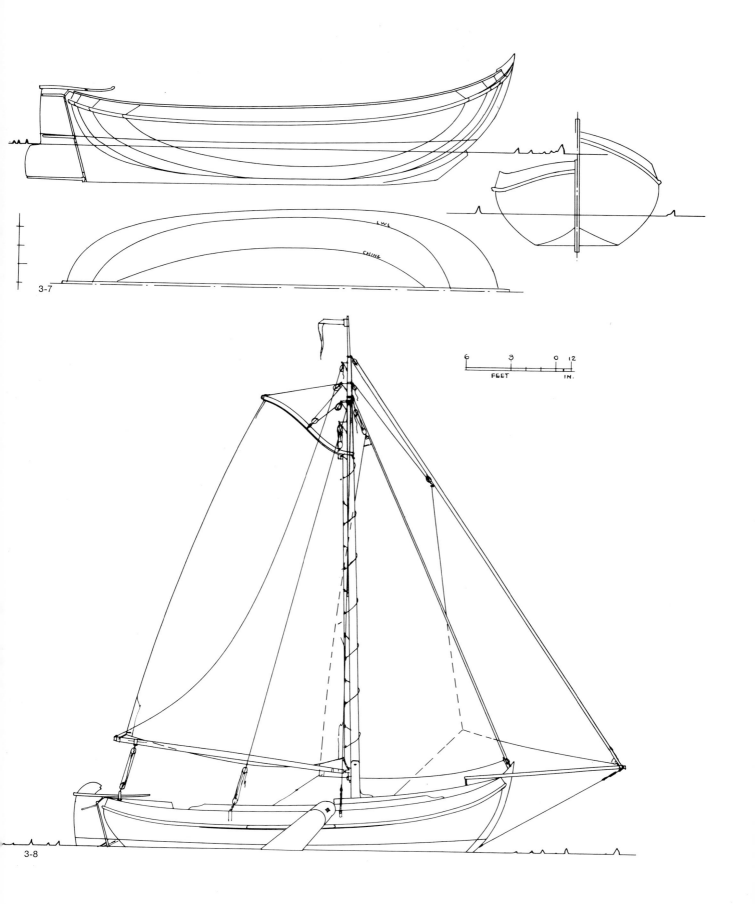

3-7

LWL

CHINE

6   3   0   12
FEET   IN.

3-8

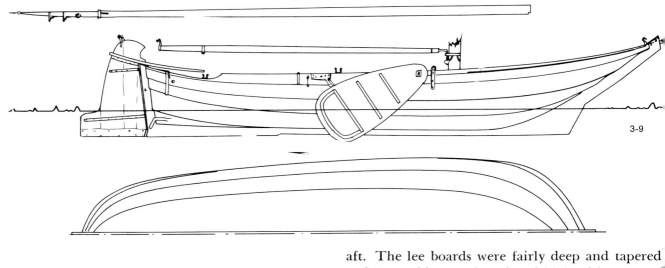

3-9

```
0   2   4   6   8   10  12
        FEET            IN.
```

3-9   The hengst is a smaller and older hoogaars still found in the Scheldt and the waters of western Holland.

3-10   The lines plan of a hoogaars. Note the flat bottom and flaring sides. This is a simple and unpretentious form.

3-11   The sail plan of a hoogaars. This is the low rig of the original working boat. The common rig now is loftier, since most of the boats have been converted to pleasure craft.

aft. The lee boards were fairly deep and tapered and the rudder was broad and high with a curved tiller sweeping down from a rudderhead that was most frequently decorated with a head, a fish, or other carving that pleased the builder or owner. In the last thirty to thirty-five years, because of the scarcity of wood, steel has been resorted to as the basic hull material, while the original form of the types was retained.

The *schokker* and the *hoogaars* are identified by their forward-raking, straight, rather than curved, stems. The schokker has a similar body form to that of the botter but with a straight stern post as well, to match its stem. The hoogaars has straight sides flaring out from a flat bottom and is generally lapstraked with three or four broad planks per side. (See Figures 3-9, 3-10, and 3-11.) Both of these craft have the characteristic tumblehome washboard plank above the sheer gunwale line which adds necessary freeboard and provides for a base on which to hinge the lee boards.

A fleet sails out of Volendam on the Ijssel Meer composed of seiners that do not have the characteristic shape of the traditional "Dutch shoe" boat. Whether these boats can be classified as indigenous is debatable. While their general form is suggestive of most North Sea boats, their rig and appurtenances are typically Dutch, to the traditional, rigid, wind vane at the masthead. These craft, with their only partially closed cabin shelter and large after wells, all painted a solid and somber black, have a round stern, straight stem, broad beam and a length of 45 to 50 feet. They have nondistinctive and graceless hulls.

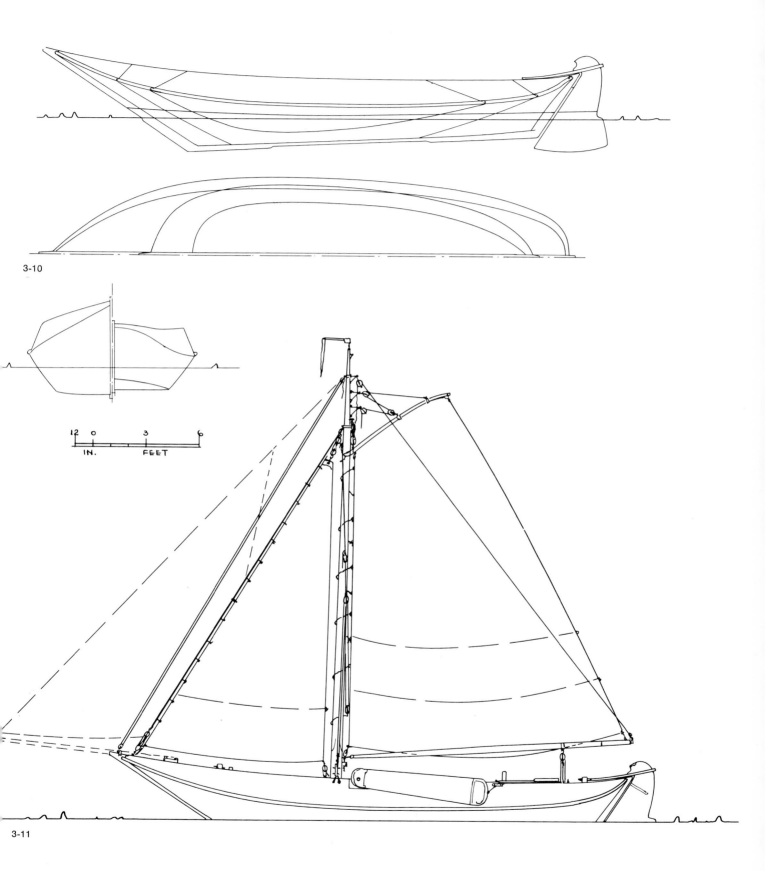

3-10

12 0   3   6
IN.   FEET

3-11

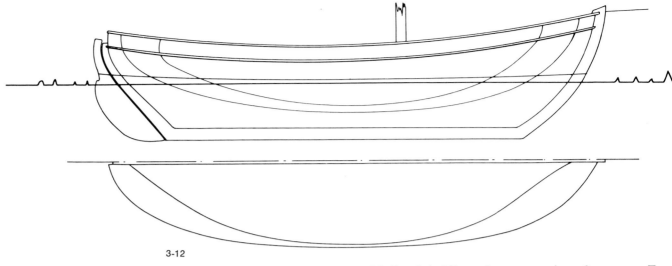

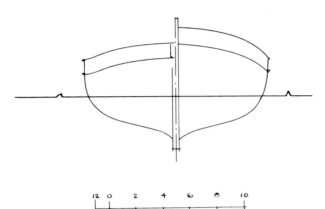

3-12

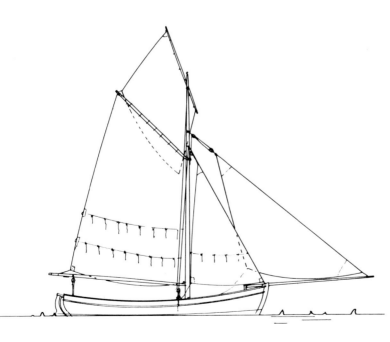

12 0 2 4 6 8 10
FEET

Holland is like other countries of western Europe, and more progressive than most, in her industrial leadership. Her modern watercraft have become large, efficient, mechanized, instrumented, professionally designed, and thoroughly modern. They are thus vessels of the modern world and no longer indigenous to the Netherlands.

Scandinavia begins just to the east of the Dutch lowlands, beyond the Frisian Islands where Jutland lies. Some of the most capable and thoroughly indigenous small sea craft sail amongst the islands of Denmark's protective peninsula, as well as in the Skaggerak and the Baltic.

Here, as elsewhere in the modern world, sail has largely given way to power. Most of today's boats, while they are borne on hulls whose lines are old and traditional, have diesel engines in place of masts and sails.

The most typical hull form used in the small, heavy workboats and fishing craft in both Danish and Swedish waters is descended from the herring and plaice fishing craft of a century or more ago. The boats employed in the vicinity of the island of Sjaelland to the north of Copenhagen, where the old fishing ports of Hornbaek and Skovshoved lie, originated the form and style found in the contemporary, small, powered fishing boats. Figure 3-12 shows the lines and rig profile of a nineteenth century fishing boat of Hornbaek; she is typically double ended, with a full heavy form, straight keel, and curving stem that is typical of the old Scandi-

3-12 *A Hornbaek sildebaaden or herring boat.*

3-13 *A small Danish coasting vessel of a type developed nearly two centuries ago to trade among the Danish Islands and in the Baltic Sea. This boat still retains her low ketch rig and has found a sympathetic owner who makes his home aboard.*

3-14 *The lines of this old Danish coaster can still be seen in Denmark's present-day coasters. These lines were drawn from those by Admiral Paris in his* Souvenirs de Marine *in 1882.*

3-13

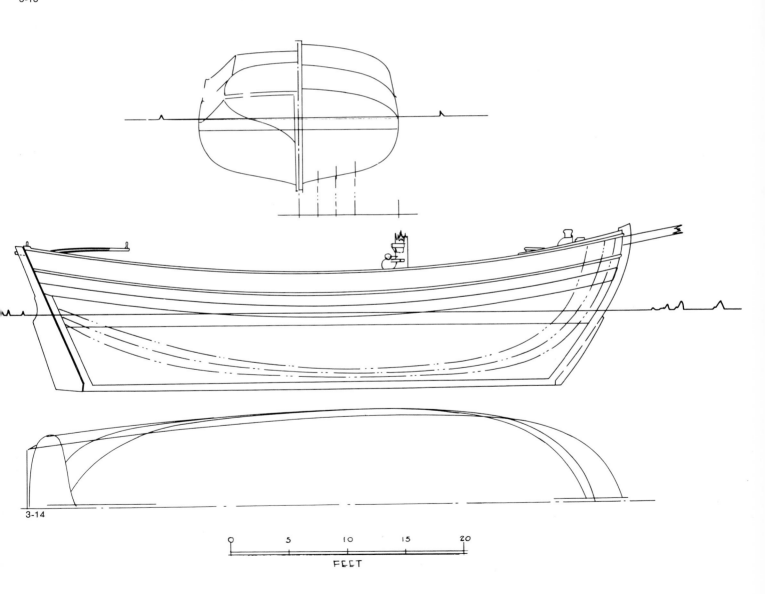

3-14

0   5   10   15   20

FEET

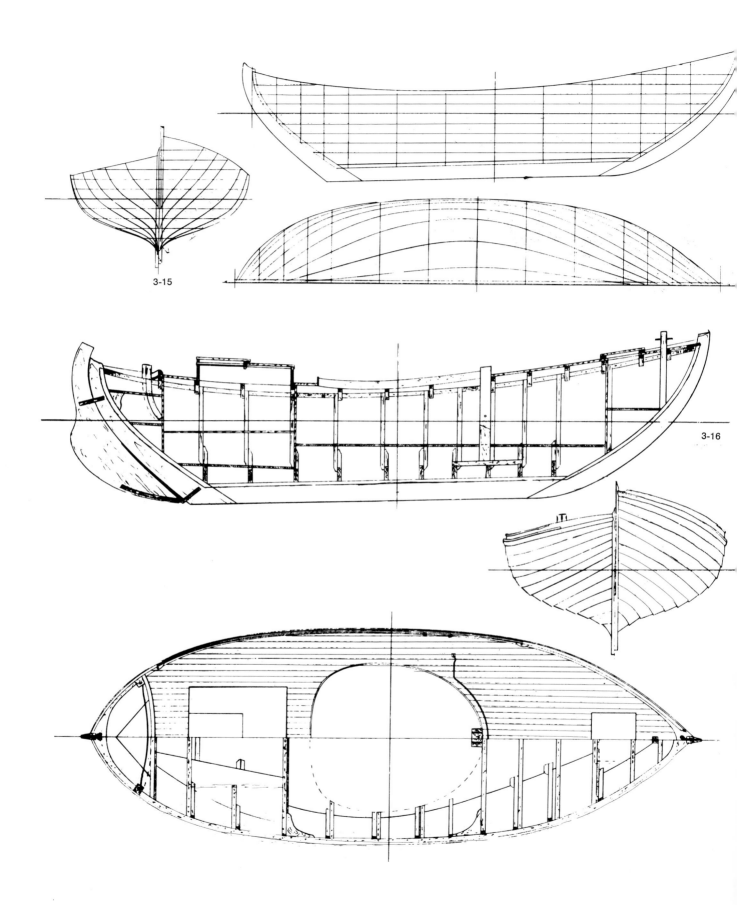

3-15

3-16

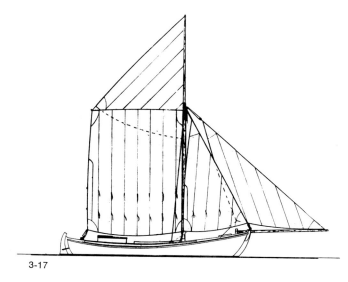
3-17

3-15   *The lines of this Skovshoved sildebaaden reflect at even a casual glance her Norse working boat influence. These boats still work the inshore fisheries but are today refitted for power.*

3-16   *The structure of this Danish herring boat is rugged and reflects ancient Norse building methods and character. She has sawn frames with an integral floor timber.*

3-17   *The sail plan of the sildebaaden is typical of all of the small Scandinavian fishing boats sailing in the Orsund for the past 100 years. Unfortunately, these rigs have given way to diesel power.*

navian style. While the hull above the water is full, her sections, both fore and aft, show a shallow wineglass form that provides a fine entrance and run below the water. The stern post is typically curved inward, also, in the Scandinavian manner. The original rig on these boats is fairly lofty, with a club topsail and two headsails and an extremely long housing bowsprit. (This was a summer rig, no doubt.) The mainsail is typically loose footed. She is 36 feet long, 13 feet in beam, and 5 feet in draft.

A larger and even older Danish boat of much this same form is shown in Admiral Paris' well-known survey. This boat is a coaster 50 feet long with a transom stern, which is quite typical of the Danish coastwise boats. Her lines and rig are otherwise quite similar indicating a well-established local form. (See Figures 3-13 and 3-14.)

The herring boats of Skovshoved, not far from Hornbaek, were a variation of the Hornbaek type. They had more grace and lightness, with a suggestion of Viking form. The lines (Figure 3-15) show a boat of smaller dimensions than the Hornbaek type, with greater curvature in the ends and with a typical old sprit rig. These boats were extremely numerous under sail in the Danish Öresund east of Copenhagen only fifty years ago. Figures 3-16 and 3-17 show the structure and sail plan of a Skovshoved boat. The construction is predominantly lapstrake, particularly in the boats of less than 40 feet.

The Danish islands as well as Jutland are rich in small rowing craft, all of them of typical Scandi-

navian mold. These craft are used today more for pleasure and recreational fishing than for commercial work. They are, however, indigenous. They vary from approximately 12 feet to 16 feet in length and are typically of lapstrake construction. They are finely modeled double-enders. Figure 3-18 indicates the size, shape, and construction of one of these rugged little beach craft.

The most unusual beach boats of Scandinavia, and perhaps the most functional contemporary beach craft anywhere, are the boats of the northeast coast of Jutland. Essentially these hard-working boats are all of similar construction and style. They are built in three sizes: small rowing boats approximately 16 feet long, open motorcraft about 20 feet long, and larger decked motorboats from 30 to 40 feet long. All of the boats are heavily constructed to withstand daily launching and beaching on coarse, steep, open strands. The beaching process is unique and complex. It is carried out cooperatively by the crews of several boats with the aid of powered winches, a cluster of anchors holding a heavy outhaul pulley block, and, on the beach, a system of fixed pulleys and a sliding pulley. The boats after being attached to the cable ride up on the beach over metal rollers (in the past, wood sleepers were used).

The boats are full bodied with lapstrake hulls. They are planked in oak with about seven planks per side for the rowing craft and with 13 planks per side for the larger decked craft. The smaller craft are similar in form to the beach craft described earlier, but the larger of the powered Jut-

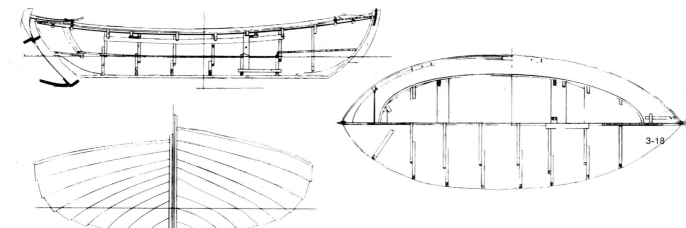

3-18

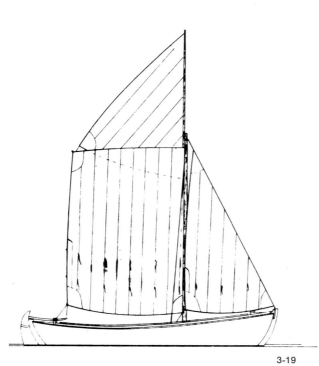

3-19

land boats are fuller amidships with a broad tran som, or with a high, full, eliptical stern as shown in Figures 3-21 and 3-22. These larger boats have a deep gunwale that provides more security to the fishermen working their hand gear on deck. There is a wheelhouse aft with access to the engine casing and engine just ahead of it. The engines of these boats, as in most Scandinavian fishing boats of this size and character, are hot-bulb semi-diesels of one two, or three cylinders. The propellers are control lable pitch because these engines have no reverse gear.

The larger, decked boats carry a standard mast and auxiliary sail rig consisting of a small gaff main and short storm jib. Figure 3-23 shows a typical profile of one of these boats whose dimensions are 37 feet overall, 14 feet beam, and 4 feet draft when loaded. Her displacement at the load waterline is about 15 tons.

These beach boats are built by local builders entirely by experience and eye. They use no draw ings or models to work from, and their boats are consequently excellent examples of indigenous art.

The scantlings of the beach boat in Figures 3-24 and 3-25 are typical. The keel is 10″ by 9″ of Dan ish oak with a steel bar shoe 3½″ by 1″. The frames are 3″ by 5″ fastened to the keel and floor timbers by natural grown knees. The planking is American oak one inch thick.

It is rather unusual to encounter beach craft in the Scandinavian countries. Where there are no convenient natural harbors and artificial harbor breakwaters are prohibitive, the use of beach craft

3-20

3-18 & 3-19   Hull lines and sail plan of a Danish Kragejolle.

3-20   This beach skiff, drawn up on the pebbled shore of the Kattegat, is typical of Danish skiffs with her fine double ends and curved-back stern post.

3-21   The klitmoller boat is distinguished by its full hull and deep sheer. It is the largest beach-launched boat of Europe with the exception of some Portuguese seiners.

3-22   The hull lines of a klitmoller boat show her full and rocker-like hull. She is comparatively flat bottomed for a lapstraked hull.

3-23   The klitmoller boat's short sail rig is used primarily today for steadying. The sail plan indicated here is representative of the present-day gaff-headed sail. The older rig still occasionally seen is the sprit.

3-21

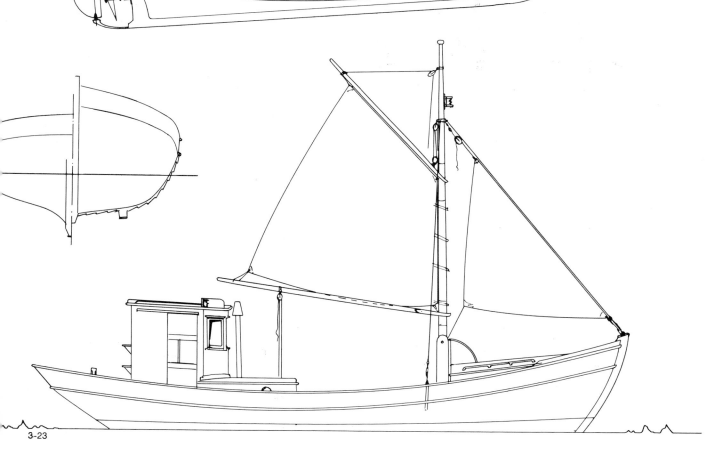

3-22

3-23

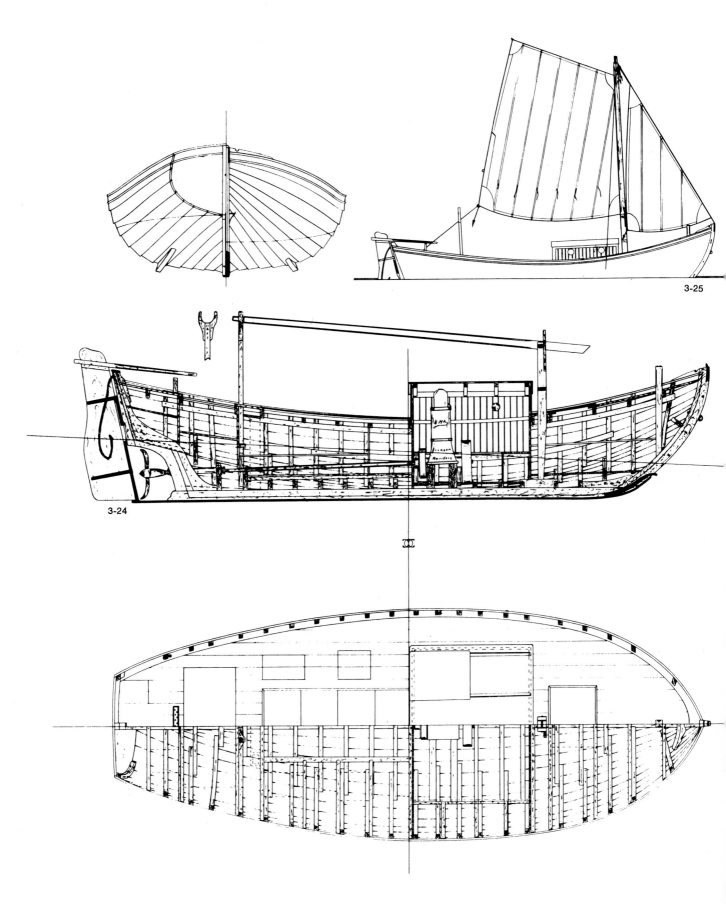

3-25

3-24

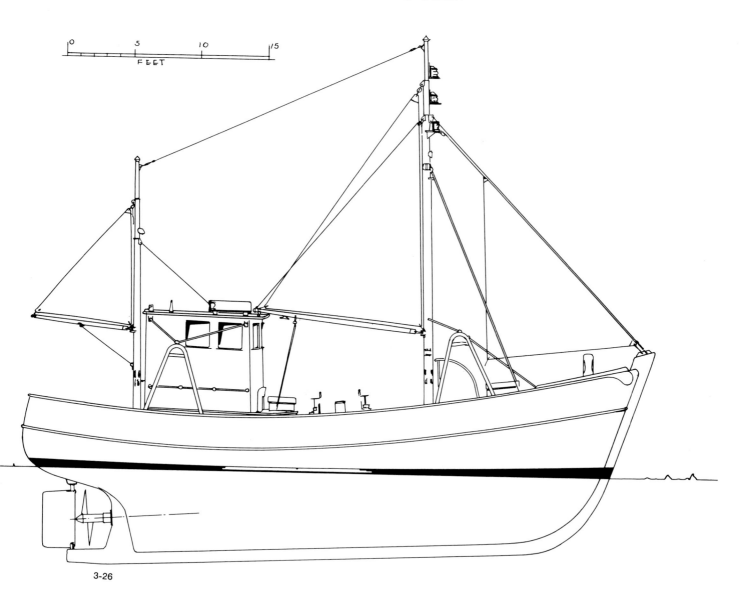

3-24 The structure of this old-style klitmoller boat shows the full hull and heavy sawn frames of Norse construction. Note the heavy beaching keels.

3-25 The outboard profile and sail plan of an old-style klitmoller boat. She measures 27' 6" length, 11' 1" beam, and 3' 9" draft. There are still a few of these older models in service.

3-26 Outboard profile of modern Danish trawler.

0   5   10   15
FEET

3-26

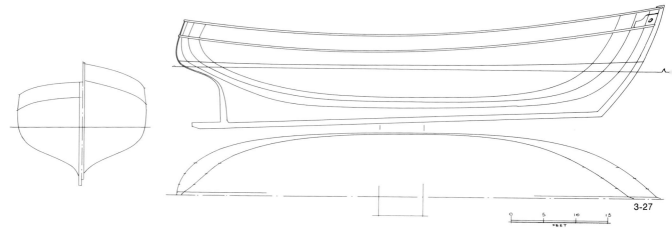

3-27

3-28

*3-27   The lines of a Swedish herring boat.
This hull is rugged but graceful, with an
inward-raking stern post and gently curving
stem.*

*3-28   The bottom of a Swedish herring boat.
Her large controllable-pitch propeller indicates
she has a heavy, low-speed diesel engine with
one forward speed.*

becomes the only solution to working the sea for
fish, providing of course there are beaches in the
area. The weather and sea are so harsh on the
Jutland coast that the days of the year fit for the
fishermen to launch their boats never number
much more than 100. The larger motorcraft can
stay at sea for several days running, but the smaller
boats as well as the larger normally fish from sun-
rise to dark.

The Scandinavian style of larger fishing craft
is used extensively in the Baltic, among the Danish islands, on the coast of Sweden, and in the more
protected waters of Norway. (The boats sailing
from the western coast of Norway to fish the North
Sea will be discussed with the North Sea boats of
other lands.) There are local variations, of course,
that to an expert eye identify not only the national
identity of the fishing craft but also their locale.
Before the variations are discussed, however, let us
look at a typical contemporary working boat of the
Scandinavian character.

This boat is first of all indigenous on a broader
scale than perhaps any other type discussed in this
book. It is indigenous to the Scandinavian protected and semi-protected waters and has its roots
in nineteenth century boats, such as those of Hornbaek and Skovshoved. The traditions behind this
boat's construction, however, began 1,000 years or
more ago with the Vikings. The most critical non-
Scandinavian must admit that they were the most
original and gifted boatbuilders in northern
Europe. A composite profile of this typically Scandinavian contemporary working boat of the fish-

3-29 *A modern Danish trawler at rest alongside a fish pier in Copenhagen. This style of Danish boat roams the North Sea and the North Atlantic as far west as Greenland.*

3-30 *This diesel-powered coaster does not disguise the fact that she was once a graceful boat powered by sail alone. She now carries cargo into the out-of-the-way ports of the Danish Islands and Swedish coast.*

3-29

eries is shown in Figure 3-26. She is approximately 45 to 50 feet in length, 16 feet in beam, and 6½ feet in loaded draft. Her loaded displacement is perhaps 75 tons.

In the fishing ports of Sweden from Göteborg to the north, many similar boats can be found. The bows of the Swedish boats are fuller with a bit more of the "apple cheeked" feeling and have stems with a continuous gentle arc. This feature is evident in the herring boats in the harbor of Honö, Sweden.

The Swedish boats in the Baltic as well as those of Denmark and Finland have similar form but crisper lines with a straighter stem. Sometimes they have two masts for steadying sails, as indicated in Figure 3-29.

In the protected waters of the Baltic there is a need for small freight carriers to trade among the islands and small ports. These boats are generally nondescript in character but have the recognizable features of nineteenth century hulls that have been converted to power. Some still have reduced masts and short bowsprits for auxiliary sail. While these boats cannot be classified according to form, they are recognizable as a type, even though they are generally loaded almost to their gunwales and their deck loads of miscellaneous crates obscure their shape.

The hulls of the Baltic coasters may be of iron or wood, and often their form is that of the Danish or Swedish schooners that were built nearly a century ago for Baltic and North Sea trade. A profile of one of these schooners is shown in Figure 3-31.

3-30

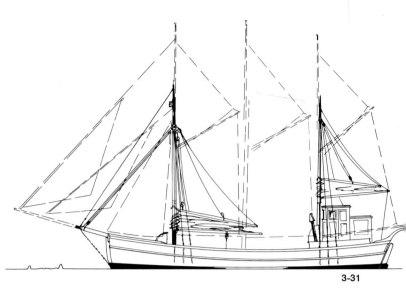

3-31 Solid lines show the profile of a present-day Baltic coaster. Dotted lines show her nineteenth-century schooner rig.

3-32 The Scandinavian pram can be found in most ports along the Skagerrak and Kattegat coasts. Her lines indicate an able and uniquely graceful boat.

3-33 The structure of this 18-foot pram is light and strong in the best Norse tradition. As a centerboarder she will perform well and efficiently to windward.

3-31

The original schooners, as the illustration shows, were three masted with topmasts, topsails, and four headsails. The mizzen, unlike on the American three-masted coasting schooners, was slightly shorter than the fore and main. Sometimes these schooners carried two or three square yards on the fore, making them a sort of topsail schooner. Their hulls, however, were typically Scandinavian, generally with transom sterns and outboard rudders. There were occassional variations with double-ended hulls. The present-day power conversions of these boats will preserve their hulls for perhaps another quarter century. Whatever their replacements will be, it is certain they will not be of such interesting, graceful, or indigenous design.

There are no evident small beach craft in Sweden, but there are many small, graceful, varnished lapstrake boats. These are used as utility craft and inshore fishing boats. Typical of these are the pram-bow craft, 12 to 15 feet long, found along the west coast of Sweden and the east coast of Denmark. These prams are found elsewhere in northern Europe as well. For instance, in England they are popular for both pleasure craft and utility boats. In Holland the blunt-bow form was first used as a variation of larger working craft and soon became popular for small rowing craft.

The Swedish-Danish version of the pram, as seen in Figures 3-32, 3-33, and 3-34, is long (about 18 feet), light, and narrow, with a bow drawn out nearly to an apex. It is a graceful lapstrake-planked craft, handy under oars or sail, with pronounced rocker in the bottom and a lifting but broad tran-

som stern. Prams are generally varnished bright, as are most of the very small craft in these waters.

As recently as fifty years ago in the Swedish, Estonian, and Finnish waters of the Baltic, there was a type of sailing workboat with pronounced Scandinavian character. The most obvious feature of these boats was their great beam, which was generally at least half of the length. Their graceful hull form, however, did not give any impression of the bulkiness often associated with such excess width. The ends were deep and fine with a body flaring upward. The boats were lapstrake planked in oak, had flush decks with an open heavy rail, and sailed under a lofty sprit rig. They were powerful sailing boats, perhaps as capable as any sailing workboat anywhere at anytime. While they are for all practical purposes now extinct, a remaining example here or there may be encountered under reduced rig and power.

The North Sea is a body of water shared by Norway, Scotland, England, and the Lowlands. It is a large gulf, really, slightly larger than the Aegean Sea but brutally exposed to the Norwegian Sea and Artic Ocean to the north. Its outlets to the south and east are the Dover Strait to the English Channel, and the Skagerrak to the Danish islands and the Baltic. This North Sea region, more than any other, proves the theory that boats assume like character from the waters they sail in and their employment. The North Sea has for centuries been one of the world's richest fisheries, and the

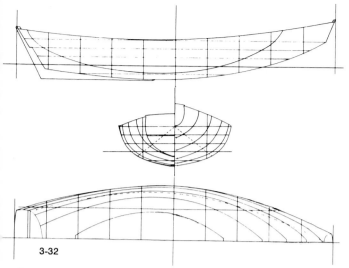

3-32

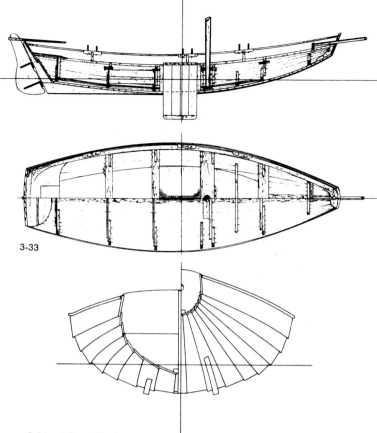

3-33

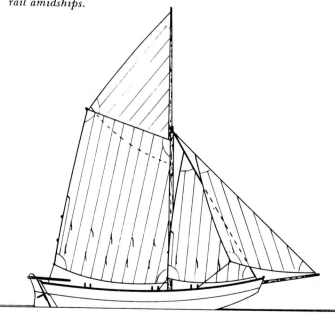

3-34   *The sail plan of the pram in Figures 3-32 & 3-33 indicates a sprit rig with a topsail and two headsails — an exceptionally well-proportioned rig. This boat measures 18 feet long, 6' 4" beam, and 2' 4" depth below her rail amidships.*

3-34

boats that have sailed it regularly have acquired similar character, as have, to an extent, the boats fishing the Grand Banks or those working in many regions of the Mediterranean. For this reason, North Sea-type boats are discussed in greater detail in the following chapter, where the Norwegian, Scottish, and British varieties of this boat type are covered.

On the Norwegian coast, which borders both the North Sea and the Norwegian Sea, ancient boatbuilding lore persists to a surprising extent in the small inshore working craft. This ancient character is strikingly evident in the inshore boats of the island-fjord region north of Bergen. The craft there are basically all that remain of the once numerous types of powerful offshore fishing and working boats of the last century and early twentieth century.

It is not surprising that Norway has contributed significantly to the finest of seagoing designs. This region of mountains and fjords was the source 1,000 years ago of the finely modeled "drakkers" of the Vikings. The skills of the Viking shipwrights directly influenced the boats of England, France, and Germany for more than 500 years. The heritage of Norway has always been the sea. Two thirds of Norway's population lives on the coastline; ninety percent of its commerce is carried on the water. The influence of Norwegian maritime knowledge and skill is most currently evident in modern ship design. The great tankers, cargo carriers, naval vessels, yachts, and even tugboats of the world bear the marks of Norwegian designers

3-35　The Nordland boat of the northwestern coast of Norway is classic. The characteristics of this boat, which descends directly from the Norse long ships of 1,000 years ago, are reflected in many lapstrake boats of Norway today. While this particular boat passed from the active scene about two decades ago, there are smaller rowing models still in use and a few larger craft similar to this are owned by fishermen in the North Islands.

3-36　The bindel boat is a small model of the Nordland boat. These can still be seen in use in the western fjords of Norway.

3-37　This natural-crook cant frame from the bow of a Norse boat of the eleventh century is identical in shape to those used in today's Norwegian skiffs and bindel boats.

3-38　This graceful Norwegian skiff reflects ancient Viking construction.

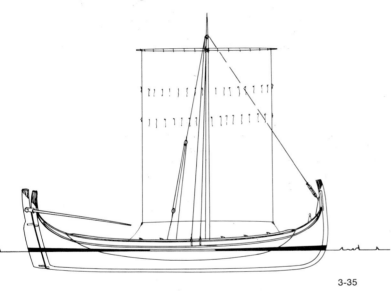

3-35

3-36

and the results of their research in their Trondheim Station for Ship Model Testing.

Only the small inshore boats of Norway, especially the rowing craft, retain characteristics of ancient design. Some of these little boats are almost miniature Viking craft. After seeing their natural-grown V-frames and their swept-up stems and sterns, one's first reaction is that they forgot the carved dragon's head. The construction is typically lapstraked, often only three planks per side in the rowing craft.

The Nordland boat, shown in Figure 3-35, is the true but practically extinct ancestor of the small, so-called Bindel boats. This boat of the nineteenth and twentieth centuries is very close to the original model developed a millenium ago. It is a small Viking coastal boat used in fishing and transport. It has a single midship mast, a square sail, six or seven oars per side, and is open from end to end with a high stem and stern post. About the only concession to modern design is a long rudder mounted on the stern post by conventional pintles and gudgeons. (The side steering oar was abandoned sometime during the thirteenth century.)

Figure 3-36 is a photograph of a Bindel boat. This particular one is 16 feet long and 5 feet wide and is built in the same ancient manner as the Nordland boat, with grown frames and knees and three planks per side below the painted sheer strake. She has the ancient Norse curved rowing pins or *kabes* instead of thole pins (a later invention).

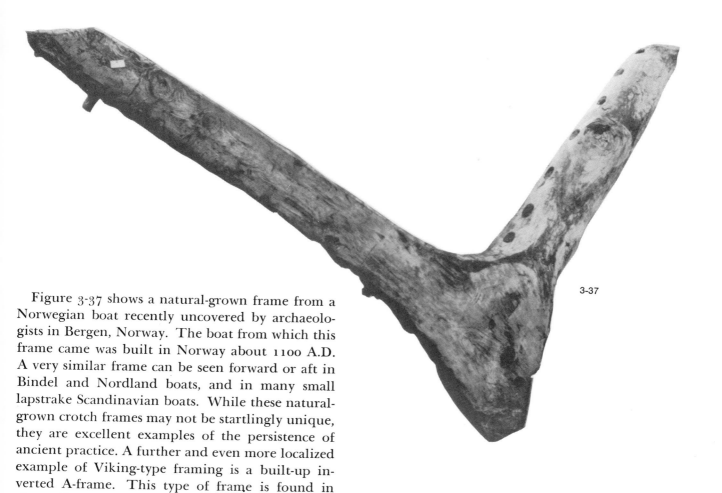

3-37

Figure 3-37 shows a natural-grown frame from a Norwegian boat recently uncovered by archaeologists in Bergen, Norway. The boat from which this frame came was built in Norway about 1100 A.D. A very similar frame can be seen forward or aft in Bindel and Nordland boats, and in many small lapstrake Scandinavian boats. While these natural-grown crotch frames may not be startlingly unique, they are excellent examples of the persistence of ancient practice. A further and even more localized example of Viking-type framing is a built-up inverted A-frame. This type of frame is found in the earliest of Viking craft and is particularly evident in the Gokstad Ship, preserved in the Oslo Museum, of 900 A.D. (See Chapter 1.) It is evident in the interior structure of the present-day Norwegian skiff in Figure 3-38.

If there is any watercraft anywhere that is reduced to the simplist *essence of a boat* it is the Norwegian coastal skiff. John Ruskin wrote about a century ago about such a boat: " . . . the bow of a boat — a common undecked sea boat, lying aside in its furrow of beach sand; the sum of navigation is in that. You may magnify it or decorate it as you will: you do not add to the wonder of it. Lengthen it into a hatchet-like edge of iron, strengthen it with a complex tracery of ribs of oak, carve it and gild it till a column of light moves beneath it on the sea, you have made no more of it than it was at first. That rude simplicity of bent plank, that can breast its way through the death that is in the deep sea, has in it the soul of shipping."

3-38

3-39

To extend this thought beyond Ruskin's bow of the boat, the Norwegian skiff has in its whole length the essence and "soul of shipping." Though this skiff has only three planks per side — often unfinished with the mill saw marks still showing — these planks are spiled and bent to form the most graceful of boat shapes. The form of the Norwegian skiff is quite consistent among the many examples that can be found along the west coast of Norway. It is most easily described by reference to Figure 3-39. It is a rakish little double-ended hull that reflects at a glance its lightness and rowability, as well as its stability and capability in rough water. There are few frames in the average skiff of this type, perhaps four at the most. The forward and aftermost frames are canted as shown in the illustration. Sometimes these boats carry a short mast with a lug sail or a loose-footed gaff sail and jib. Whether the propulsion is by oar and ancient hooked thole, or by sail, the boat is always most simple and functional. If there is such a thing as the "basic boat," it must be here.

Aside from the erosive effects of time and the gradual changes of economy and technology, the factor most destructive to small indigenous workboats has been the great wars that have swept northern Europe in this century. Both World Wars I and II combined to eliminate effectively the most picturesque as well as capable sailing workboats of the continental English Channel coast. The small luggers that sailed out of the fishing ports of Brittany, Normandy, and Flanders are now gone. They were doubtless doomed anyway, but would have lingered perhaps a while longer had not they and their industry been overwhelmed by the violence of war. These craft were sunk by passing gunboats and U-boats and were commandeered by invading troops. It was not profitable to replace them with boats of the same form and rig. The fisheries of Belguim are now served by modern boats of larger and more efficient design. The inshore fisheries of the French coast are no longer productive for smaller craft. There are thus no longer any boats on this coast that can be described as indigenous.

Before passing over the Channel to the working boats of the British Islands in the following chapter, it might be appropriate simply to illustrate a former boat of the Brittany coast as a respectful tribute to the seagoing tradition of this region. Figure 3-40 is a profile of a French *chasse-marée* or sea hunter. The profile of this boat shows the character of these powerful luggers. This boat is most representative of the feeling and character in all of the sailing workboats of the northern French and Flemish coasts that operated until the early part of the twentieth century. It cannot be possible that the traditions and skills of indigenous boatbuilders were lost when these boats ceased to exist. Their sailing rigs are gone but some of their form and line are still a part of an occasional contemporary boat found sailing from Brittany or even built in Belgium for export, as some modern trawlers are. Indigenous tradition, for the most part, is immortal.

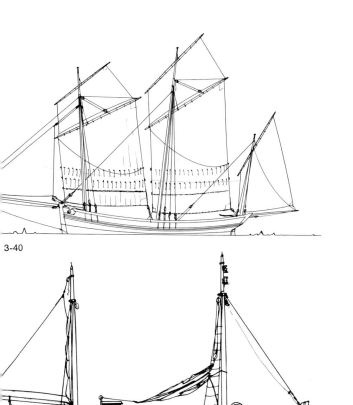
3-40

3-41

3-42

3-39   The Norwegian skiff shares its heritage with modern Scottish and Icelandic small boats. As in the Viking skiffs, there are only three planks to a side and but five interior frames.

3-40   The classic profile of a chasse marée of Brittany on the French coast of the English Channel. This boat is the origin of much of the rugged construction and hull form of today's modern French and Flemish trawlers. These boats originated in the early nineteenth century and continued to be used until World War II.

3-41   The profile of a powered fishing craft of the French coast of the English Channel. Many of the older boats are converted luggers, though the more recently constructed boats follow the same basic form and profile. The similarity of this hull with that of the chasse marée is evident.

3-42   This modern fishing boat of Normandy is rugged in the tradition of the old plumb-stemmed luggers.

4 / WORKING CRAFT OF THE BRITISH ISLANDS

BRITISH MARITIME CULTURE has its roots in the Norse culture of the Vikings, which was first introduced to the British Islands by William the Conqueror in the middle of the eleventh century.

William, Duke of Normandy, was descended from Rollo the Viking, who had conquered and colonized Normandy a few generations before William was born. The Normans, whose name was derived from *Norsemen,* brought their crafts, skills, and aggressive instincts from Scandinavia to the shores of northern France. In this Dutchy of Normandy, for the few generations before William became the Duke, the new settlers accommodated themselves to the climate, culture, and language of the Franks. They did not, however, lose their skill and knowledge of boatbuilding. Nor did they forget how to use them in equipping an expedition to foreign shores.

In a single, amphibious maneuver, William of Normandy landed seven thousand men on the English shore at Pevensey. Accompanying this horde of knights and soldiers were 3,000 horses, together with an arsenal of weapons, armor, and supplies to sustain a protracted invasion. The boats that carried this formidable amphibious conquest were Viking-type *long ships,* authentic down to their decorative dragon heads and tails at stems and sterns, striped and otherwise decorated single square sails, shields along the gunwales, and long curved steering oars. The boats crossed the Channel at night under sail, for William wisely waited for a favorable wind rather than prematurely exhaust his men at the oars. Most of the boats were

fitted with 32 oars. They were built of lapstrake oak planks by skilled Norman shipwrights at the mouth of the River Dives on the Norman coast. There is no reason to believe that these ships were different in size, shape, and construction from those that had been used by Viking raiders and Norman settlers for the several hundred years prior to William's invasion. They were long ships like those which have been found intact or nearly so in modern Norway and Denmark and can be seen today.

William's ships are illustrated in a remarkable work commemorating his conquest. The invasion story is told on a 231-foot hand-woven tapestry 20 inches wide that was woven at the bidding of William's wife, Matilda. This tapestry illustrates the actions of Duke William from the time he was promised the English throne by King Edward the Confessor to his bloody victory over King Harold at Hastings. This original picture-history can be seen today in the city of Bayeux in the French province of Normandy. On it can be seen the boats being built for the conquest, their provisioning, their channel crossing, and their landing.

Before William's conquest, England was ruled piecemeal by jealous Saxon lords who were unable to prevent frequent landings and pillagings by aggressive Danish raiders. Many of these raiders chose to settle, and a succession of Danish and Saxon kings sat on uneasy thrones. William consolidated these factions in the eleventh century, and England became a unified nation of seaconscious people.

4-1

4-2

The boats and later ships that were developed were to follow the solid, no-nonsense structure of the boats of the Norsemen. These boats had a fine entrance at the waterline with hollow forefoot, flaring bows, and a lifting sheer line. In the centuries that followed, they led to a multiplicity of types of small craft and a number of cumbersome larger craft, ordered, no doubt, by seapower-conscious monarchs.

We must look at the environment surrounding the British Isles, including the North Sea, as we examine specific British small craft. The British Isles, in the context of this chapter, refers, of course, to the waters surrounding England, Scotland, and Ireland as well as the small island groups such as the Shetlands, Hebrides, and Faeroes. The political and geographical boundaries within this region are of minor importance to this study.

At the northern limits of this region, the coast of Scotland on the North Sea is closer to the fjords of Norway than to London or the southern shores of England. It is natural that common working of the rich North Sea fisheries should bring about some similarities between Norwegian and Scottish craft.

The small working boats of Scotland and the east coast of England have been influenced through history almost totally by the fortunes of the herring industry. Salt-cured herring has been a staple of diet for the people of northern Europe for at least a millennium, and for several centuries this industry was dominated by the thrifty Dutch. Until

King Charles I in the seventeenth century demanded the large fee of £30,000 from Holland for the privilege of catching the fish near the English and Scottish coasts, neither the English nor the Scots had engaged seriously in this industry. Until then, the fishermen of Britain had only fished inshore from small open boats to provide for their own families or, at most, local communities. Their boats were similar to the Norwegian skiffs and Nordland boats described in Chapter 3. They were open boats of lapstrake construction, propelled by oars or a very simple sailing rig. Such boats have prevailed in isolated regions in small numbers until now, especially in the islands north of Scotland. However, the demand for herring brought on the Anglo-Dutch wars of the seventeenth century and ultimately resulted in the development of larger fishing craft supporting a thriving industry from the bays and firths of Scotland.

By the nineteenth century these Scottish-built fishing craft dominated the coastal and offshore fisheries in the British North Sea waters and were sheltered from any serious foreign threat by the great navy of the British Empire. The boats were of many categories but were generally two-masted, lug-rigged sailing craft varying in length from 35 to 70 feet. Many of them were unattractive, marginal-design products of builders with limited skills. On the other hand there were a few types "designed" and built by craftsmen of considerable capability. These boats were to be the ones that prevailed and survived the transition from sail to power.

4-1 Norwegian influence is clearly evident in the character of this late nineteenth-century herring boat model.

4-2 The Shetland ness yole was simply an enlarged version of the Norway skiff. The component parts were often imported from Norway, prefabricated.

4-3 The North Isles yole, a harbor and coastal boat, is almost a direct descendent of the Norse craft.

4-3

4-4 The Scottish zulu was essentially a fifie with an extreme rake to the stern post. This same type of hull with the raked stern post is still evident in some trawlers of Scotland and Ireland today.

4-5 The sixern was a heavier boat than the ness yole and operated farther off shore. Sixerns were about 32 feet in length and 10 feet in beam, and were lapstrake planked of fir in the Norwegian manner and iron fastened. They were used extensively until the beginning of this century for deepsea line and net fishing and carried a single, dipping lug sail. They contributed, together with the other Scottish boats of this and related character, to the well known fifie type and, later, to the contemporary trawler.

4-6 The outboard profile and lines of a Scottish fifie. This boat, when mechanically powered, became the prototype for the later modern wooden trawlers and ring netters.

4-5

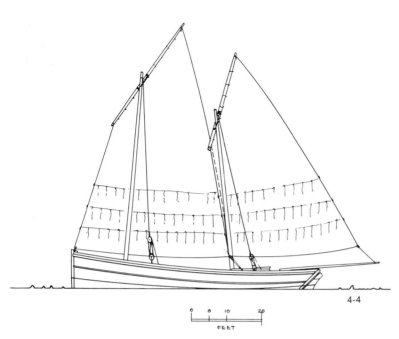

4-4

FEET

Before describing these present-day power craft, the smaller open fishing boats that preceded the upturn in the herring fishery industry should be described. In the Shetland Islands and the Orkneys and south as far as Moray Firth, a type of open fishing boat called a sixern established a notable reputation. The name refers to the boat's complement of six oars. Its style and configuration was definitely Norse, being clinker-built with upswept stem and stern sheer lines similar to Nordland boats. These boats evolved into larger craft and ultimately, in the nineteenth century, became known as scaffies. At the same time the enlargement of many Scottish harbors and the population growth as a result of the industrial revolution brought greater demands on the fisheries, and larger decked boats were built. These larger fishing craft lacked most of the Norse or Viking flavor of the earlier small craft but still retained the double-ended form and the lug-sail rig. The most predominant type was called a fifie. The predominant features of a fifie were its "melon-seed" double-ended hull, nearly vertical stem and stern and rather flat sheer profile. (See Figure 4-6.) I do not think that they were distinguished by their beauty; however, a fleet of them running for harbor with a fresh catch in a North Sea gale should have been a most impressive sight.

These boats and similar craft performed most ably for nearly three-quarters of a century in the North Sea herring industry. As a matter of fact, this entire North Sea enterprise continued to bring an ever-increasing wealth. At the turn of the cen-

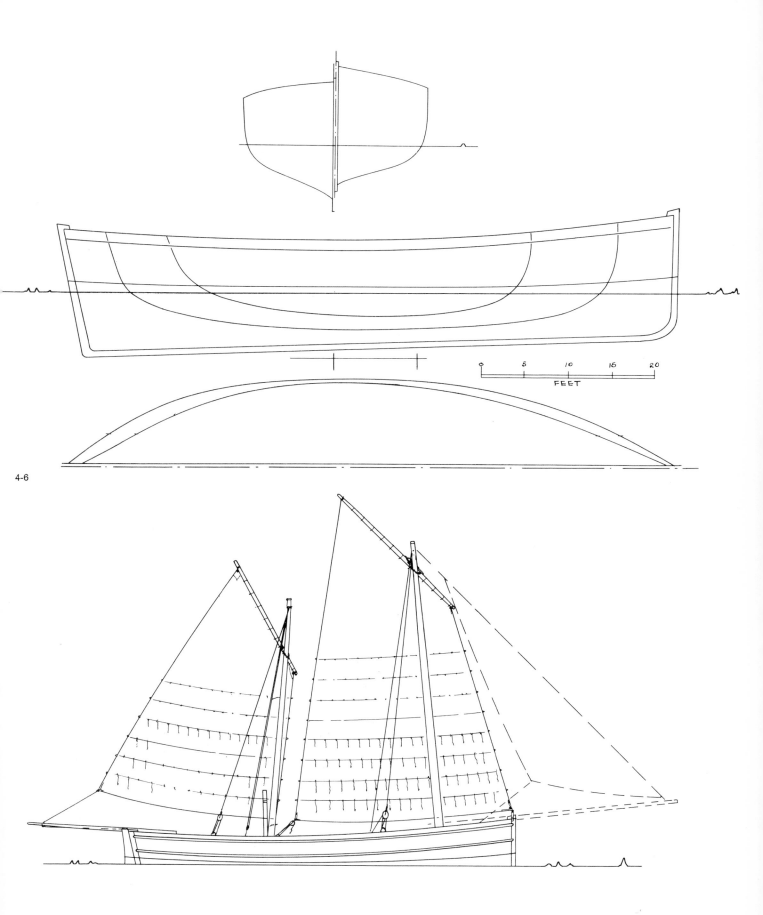

4-6

4-7   This large, powerful Scottish trawler measures 60 feet by 19 feet and is powered by a 240 h.p. diesel. She was built in 1965.

4-8   The contemporary Scottish ring netter is a most powerful and impressive boat. In this fine example built by Miller and Sons of St. Monance, Fife, Scotland in 1966, the strong Norse heritage is still evident in her sweeping sheer, the rise of her stem, and her fine entrance. She is 58 feet long overall and 18½ feet in beam.

4-9   This Norwegian seiner is very similar in style to the Scottish model. This similarity is the result of the need to perform the same function in the same environment and is not necessarily the result of imitation.

4-7

4-8

tury there were no less than eight distinct types of sailing herring drifters operating from Scottish and English harbors, with the Scottish boats predominating in size and number. The largest were the Scotch fifie and a similar craft called the zulu which was basically a large fifie with the raked stern post of the scaffie. Such boats were up to nearly 80 feet in length. With the introduction of power to the drifters and trawlers, steam power predominated, but finally diesel power became universal.

The first motor fishing vessels were actually fifie-type hulls with a short steadying sail rig on two masts. The subsequent development of fishing gear and improved methods brought a new type of net called the ring net, which made catching herring simpler and more dependable. This development in turn brought a fundamental change in hull design, primarily because handling the ring net required a more maneuverable, quick-turning boat. The outboard rudder and extreme aft location of the propeller used on boats of the fifie-type hull were awkward and unresponsive, and the propeller broke water frequently in a seaway. Consequently the canoe stern or modified cruiser stern was adopted. Boats of this configuration, as illustrated in Figures 4-7 and 4-8, are the basic, indigenous North Sea herring fish-boats of today. They sail from Scottish, English, and Norwegian harbors as well as from many Dutch and Belgian ports.

In this industry boats are generally becoming larger. Their more sophisticated designs and steel hulls (often if they are Dutch) consequently de-

4-9

stroy their indigenous character. However, the Scottish and Norwegian boats hold closely to the old traditions. They are built of wood, largely pitch pine on oak frames. The Norwegian boats invariably have bright-varnished hulls showing the yellowish wood-grained planks. They also carry a white stripe at the sheer below the rail from stem to stern. The only characteristic difference between these North Sea boats and those from Bergen and Stavanger and other Norwegian ports is the straighter stem post of the North Sea boats. Norwegian herring drifters have decks that are quite wide forward, which produces a flaring bow, and sometimes they have a counter stern and large deckhouse aft. Essentially they are indigenous to the North Sea and have established a reputation over the world for their seaworthiness and handiness in foul weather.

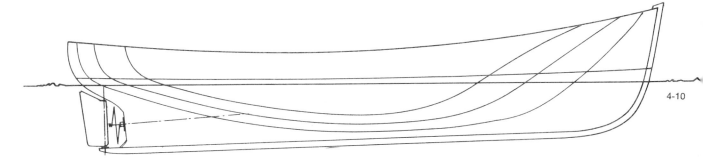

4-10

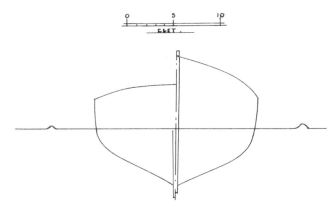

To better illustrate the hull configuration and proportions of these splendid North Sea boats, the hull lines of a typical Scottish ring netter are reproduced in Figure 4-10. These modified lines have been redrawn from a tank test report provided through the Food and Agriculture Fishing Boat Section of the United Nations. This North Sea boat was built in 1945 in Dumbarton, Scotland. Her dimensions are 62 feet overall, 17.4 feet beam, and 7.21 feet draft aft. She is powered by a four-cylinder diesel engine developing about 140 horsepower, which produces a top speed of about 10 knots. Note that there is a definite flattening in the run from amidships to the quarter. The bow sections show a nice flare, and a full deck line carried out to the stem indicates a dry hull.

I had occasion several years ago to tank-test a hull very much like this one in a series of rough-water tests comparing her with a more sophisticated and more contemporary trawler hull. The newer hull had a more rakish stem with a fuller stern and finer waterlines. There were other subtle differences in coefficients that would only have significance to a naval architect. Needless to say, but surprising to the students conducting the tests, the older boat proved markedly superior in waves that were progressively increased in height. She was able to hold a modest cruising speed in waves that would have required the more modern boat to heave to, with both boats loaded similarly. Throughout the entire sets of wave spectrums in which the tests were conducted, the power required for equivalent speeds was less for the Scot-

4-10   The hull form of a typical Scottish ring
netter is shown in this drawing of the
lines profile. This hull is taken from the
compilation of towing tank tests by the Food
and Agriculture Organization, Fishing Boat
Section. The boat was built in Dunbarton,
Scotland, in 1945.

4-11   Boats of the Faeroe Islands show the
character and detail of ancient Norse
construction, but at the same time retain their
own individuality. The Faeroe islanders are
direct descendents of Viking colonists who
settled in the Faeroes during the ninth and
tenth centuries. Until recent years, they had
little trade with the outside world.

4-11

tish herring drifter. A modern designer would be
well advised to look closely at this boat's form if
it is an able sea-boat hull he is to create. It is not
difficult, for one accustomed to studying hull lines,
to see the obscured reflection of an old Norse hull
in this Scottish boat. This basic hull form persists with slight variations throughout the British
Isles, and may be seen in some boats of North
America.

To uncover the purest indigenous boats, those
which reflect the ancient forms with the least ob-
scurity, it is necessary to look to the most isolated
communities—communities where the people live
in environments remote from contemporary society. The most fruitful locales are usually islands,
displaced from the trails of commerce and the
technological paraphanalia so common to twentieth century civilization. Such communities are becoming increasingly rare, but one such still thrives
in the seas north of Scotland, equidistant from
Norway, Iceland, and Scotland. This is the small
archipelago of the Faeroes.

The Faeroes were occupied more than a thousand years ago by Norsemen following their Viking raiding parties. It is said that the Vikings
drove out or killed the Celtic monks who first settled in the seventh century as a recluse order.
There are still ruins of an ancient and forgotten
abbey there. The Faeroese of today are unmistakably the decendants of the early Norse settlers,
and their lives, their habits, and their traditions
of dress bear striking similarity to the old Danish

and Norwegian styles. While their culture is not
primitive, they have adapted to a life style caused
by centuries of self sufficiency. While, also, they
have been a part of the Kingdom of Denmark for
many hundreds of years, they speak a language of
their own more similar to that of the ninth and
tenth century Norse than to any modern Scandinavian tongue. Although their diet is varied and
somewhat similar to other Scandinavian diets,
their most basic staples are air-cured mutton, sea
birds and their eggs, and processed whale blub-
ber, which is a delicacy. Until only recently in
this century, their homes were of rugged old stone
with sod roofs. It is natural to expect that the boats
used by these people would have much in common
with the boats that the Norsemen first brought to
these shores 1,000 years ago, and this is the case;
today's Faeroese boats are practically the same in
structure and form as the ancient Viking craft.
They are similar to the shapely Norwegian skiff
but have a greater variation in size, from 12 feet to
nearly 40. They carry two to eight oars, and have
eight to thirteen lapped strakes per side. These
Faeroese boats have retained a purity of ancient
style that is unique.

A typical eight-oared boat used in the inshore
fisheries is nearly 35 feet overall on a beam of
eight feet. (See Figure 4-11.) She is lapstrake
planked over sawn double frames widely spaced,
and is undecked even to the ends, with stem and
stern post elevated about twelve inches above the
sheer line. Both the stern post and the stem post
are curved in profile from keel to head.

4-12

4-13

Some Faeroese boats carry an outboard rudder but a steering oar is common. They do not have the extreme upswept sheer in their ends reminiscent of the Viking long boats, but instead have the more natural, lively sheer of the old Norse working boats, and perhaps of the ancient knorrs, which were tenth- and eleventh-century Norse trading boats. These boats, needless to say, are superb boats in rough water. Their origins are basically the same as the small beach craft and inshore boats of Denmark, the skiffs of Norway, the transplanted lapstrake boats of Nova Scotia, and the New England whaleboats of the past century.

In a number of the Faeroese boats, an outboard motor is often observed sputtering in a central well cut into the hull alongside the keel. The lines and structure of the boat are intact, but I wonder how long these sailors, accustomed to oars, will live with this smelly, noisy mechanism before becoming aware that it is more efficient at the stern of a flatter bottomed hull.

On the North Sea coast of England, there are few genuine indigenous craft, and those that remain are slowly becoming extinct. This coast, as well as the rest of the British coast, not too long ago was the home of a multitude of sailing workboat types. Now it is a region of small working powerboats that cannot be categorized. Most of these boats are modern examples of independent or experimental design that have lost all traces of heritage. There are some, however, that show the influence of Scottish builders and are variations of the powerful North Sea drifter type described previously. The skills of Scotland's building yards have been used extensively by the English for centuries. Scottish yards have built craft ranging from the largest Cunard ships to the smallest fishing boats.

The smaller fishing boats used for prawning, lobstering, and scallop dredging are essentially smaller versions of the same hulls as those of the herring drifter and even larger trawlers. They average about 30 feet in length and are double-ended beamy hulls with diesel engines of about 30 h.p. A typical Scottish type used for lobstering is illustrated in Figures 4-12 and 4-13. She was built in St. Monance, Fife, Scotland for a fisherman of Bournemouth, England. She is 28 feet long, 10 feet in beam, and 3 feet in draft, and is powered by a 28 h.p. diesel. Built in 1965 of larch planking on oak frames, she has a large, roomy well deck with a combined wheelhouse and engine aft. She has a single mast with steadying sail which, unlike the triangular sail on Danish craft of similar style, is a regular gaff sail. This type of boat reflects the best and most traditional in Scottish building. Her appearance alone, with well-formed hull and natural sheer line, heavy rails, and a straight-reaching stem head, projects an air of sea-going confidence to any observer. These boats are affectionately referred to as "pot haulers."

A similar inshore English craft typical of the Cornish coast, long renowned for its sailors, is shown in Figure 4-14. This boat is slightly larger than the one described above; she is 36 feet long, 11 feet 8 inches in beam, and 4 feet 6 inches in

4-12 & 4-13   This small, rugged Scottish boat is locally known as a pot hauler. Anywhere else she would be called a lobsterboat. Her heavy construction is similar to her larger sister, the Scottish ring netter, as they are both descended from the same sailing drifters. She was built in St. Monance in 1965 with larch planking on an oak frame. She is 28 feet long, 10 feet in beam, and 3 feet in draft. She is powered by a 28 h.p. diesel.

4-14   The coast of Cornwall in England is renowned for its sailors and tough, sea-going boats. This boat from Penzance is quite typical of the present-day Cornish fishing craft that replaced the plumb-stemmed luggers. Note the straight sheer and vertical, square transom stern with outboard rudder.

4-14

4-15 A Cornish oyster dredger under sail. This boat carries her summer canvas with a square-headed jackyard topsail. She was built as an open lugger about 50 years ago. Like the Chesapeake skipjacks, these oyster boats participate in an annual race to open the season. In England, however, the prize is a keg of ale.

4-16 A Cornish lugger that has been converted to power. She originally had two masts.

draft. She is similar to a majority of English-built workboats, showing some of her own, rather than Scottish, regional influence. The most dominating feature of British building evident immediately in this boat is the over-all restraint. To the eye of a naval architect, the boat seems to lack the natural flow and shape of the sea that was so easy for the Norsemen to introduce so long ago and pass on to a considerable degree to the Scots. To use an apt description common among American yacht designers when confronted with a boat impressing them as this type does me: "She looks as though she hasn't been taken out of the box she came in." A description as disparaging as this deserves qualification.

These boats of Cornwall and elsewhere along the south coast of Britain are sturdy craft. They differ from Scottish boats primarily in their flat sheer line and square transom stern. Their stems are quite plumb and their entrances and runs are fuller than those of Scottish-built boats. Boats such as these are of traditional Cornish design and are suitable for all types of inshore fishing. The hull of our example in Figure 4-14 is of round-bilge form, carvel planked, and built to the most exacting and conservative specifications. Her keel and backbone structure are of oak, and her planking is of larch. Her fastenings are either copper or galvanized steel, and her frames are natural grown-to-shape oak. Her decks and cabin structure are clear pine. She is fitted with a heavy, wood outboard rudder, protective rub rails, and steel stem and keel shoe. Her engine is an 85 h.p. Rolls-Royce

diesel, which produces a speed of eight to nine knots. She is a proper little fishing boat typical of the best British sea-going tradition. As such, she must be recognized as an indigenous type, as were her forbears — the Cornish luggers of the past century. They too were fine, ruggedly built boats, that had similar flat sheers, plumb stems, flat bows, and boxy sterns. They did not sail as well as they should or were said to have.

4-

4-16

There still are some interesting workboats under sail that survive on the English coasts. On the Cornish coast in the Carrick Roadstead, a stretch of water reaching inland from Falmouth, there is a type of small gaff cutter that survives as an oyster dredger. It "survives" much in the same manner that the Chesapeake skipjack survives — under protective conservation laws prohibiting the dredging of oysters by powered fishing boats. The oyster industry is so favorable at present that many new boats are even being built for the business. About 20 to 30 boats are at work during the season. There is no "fixed" boat type here except in rig. Most boats are between 25 and 30 feet in length with transom sterns and plumb stems. They have, most of them, the characteristic shape (or lack of it) described above for other Cornish boats. In fact there is good reason to believe, from the age of many of the boats and their hull styles, that they were formerly part of the fleet of fishing luggers sailing out of the Cornish coves at the turn of the century. The original rig of these luggers was most often two-masted, with short lug sails and no jib. Whether this was the origin of the oyster boats or not is open to question. A Cornish lugger that has been converted to power is seen in Figure 4-16.

At present the oyster boat rig is essentially that of the celebrated English gaff cutter. The long horizontal bowsprit, with two head sails, and the well-peaked gaff set on a mast stepped nearly amidships produces this handsome and well-proportioned nineteenth century cutter. The jib is set flying and in this oyster boat, while working the

beds, is frequently slacked down onto the bowsprit, and the main is reefed. Dredging with reduced sail is not, as often assumed, a shortening of sail because of foul weather, but rather it is to hold down the dredging speed and prevent the dredge from jumping along over the oyster bed.

The small sailing oyster smacks, while not uniform in size or hull characteristics, are sufficiently similar to be categorized. They are most similar in appearance to a former type of this same region that was a most noteworthy boat. The Falmouth quay punt, of which there are none still at work and perhaps less than a half dozen still extant as pleasure craft conversions, was a fine workboat. (It may be worth noting that I designed and owned a modified quay-punt a number of years ago which I sailed about the Chesapeake for several years with a great deal of pleasure.)

The Falmouth quay punt was generally an open craft with a gaff yawl rig and two head sails. Her hull was about 25 feet in length and 8 feet in beam with a plumb stem and a transom stern. She was employed carrying stores and ferrying passengers to and from the large square-rigged ships lying-to off Falmouth or anchored in the roadstead. However, these fast little boats differed in an important respect other than in their rig from the fishing luggers of this locality. Their hull sections had a nice wine-glass shape, which, with their relatively light, buoyant body, gave them a good bearing on the water. Figure 4-18 shows a model of an old quay punt in her winter rig. The summer rig was the same rig with the addition of a long bowsprit

4-17

4-18

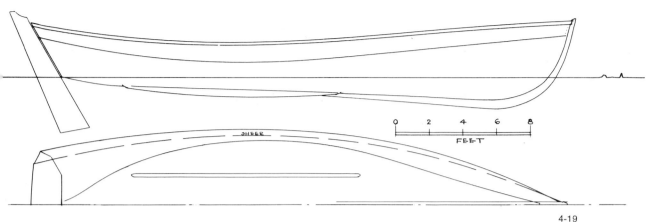

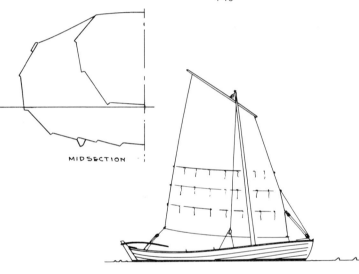

4-19

4-17 shows a quay punt in her summer rig in the early part of this century.

and large jib. Figure 4-17 shows a quay punt in her summer rig in the early part of this century.

Still another, but radically different, sailing workboat (now seen very infrequently with sail) is the Yorkshire coble. The coble, found on the east coast of England is a close relative of the older sailing Scottish skiffs but is larger, being from 25 to 30 feet in length. These boats are essentially beach boats, launched and landed in the surf, and they reflect this application. Figure 4-19 indicates the basic shape of these boats as well as their lug rig, which is nicely proportioned but not often seen now. Their hulls are heavily built of lapstrake planking, with flat aftermost sections and a hollow entrance. Figure 4-20 shows the heavy beaching keels; however, there is now a tendency for the owners of these craft to keep them lying at moorings whenever possible.

The notable characteristics of the cobles that distinguish them from their Scottish relatives, now gone, are the tumblehome of the sheer plank and the absence of a continuous external keel. A "ram

4-17   A Falmouth quay punt under summer rig. A number of these punts have been converted to pleasure craft and still sail. They are the prototypes of many of the present Falmouth oyster-dredging sloops that are still being built in the old manner.

4-18   A model of a Falmouth quay punt in her winter rig.

4-19   The lines and sail plan of a Yorkshire coble, a lug-rigged workboat that still survives.

4-20   This model clearly shows the unique bottom form of the Yorkshire coble. Today's cobles still operate occasionally from the beach, but they are heavy boats and are fitted now with diesel engines. The owners of modern cobles are more inclined to moor them in the harbor than to haul them out on the beach.

4-20

plank," which is thicker than the other planks, substitutes for the central keel aft of amidships. In the forebody, it is worked into the conventionally shaped keel and stem. Some cobles have flat, raking, transom sterns, as in Figure 4-20, and some are double-ended. These latter variants are called "mules." All cobles have a deep, narrow rudder that must be rigged after launching. These unique boats have been used in the Yorkshire lobster and inshore fishing industry for more than a century and sail out of such ports as Scarborough, Flamborough, and Whitby. They were fast and capable in the hands of the experienced skipper, but tricky and dangerous for the unwary sailor. Nowadays they are mostly powered by gas engines.

Hastings, on England's south coast, has a steep pebble beach where another unique working boat survives in an environment uninviting to more normal craft. The Hastings lugger is a deep and full lapstrake boat. It has two masts with a reduced lug-sail rig, considerable beam, and most unusual mechanical power arrangements. This boat, while faintly charming, can best be described as eccentric. The means of propulsion provide for almost any contingency. The boats are fitted with two to three propellers driven by diesel or gas engines or both, with widely differing horsepower.

The Hastings lugger of the eighteenth and early nineteenth centuries, which is very similar in hull and rig to the boat of today, was used primarily in service and rescue work for larger vessels in trouble off the beaches of Hastings and Deal. The boats were maintained in constant readiness for launch-

4-21 The Hastings lugger of today is still the same basic boat as that of the eighteenth century. Note her easily stepped rig, protected propeller, and high freeboard. This boat still operates from the beaches of Hastings and Deal and is even seen occasionally on the beaches of the French side of the Channel.

ing into the surf, and their state of reliability was the chief concern of their owners. It is reasonable to assume that this penchant for dependable functioning has carried over to the present-day types and owners.

A typical Hastings lugger shown in Figure 4-21 displaces 7½ tons, and is 28 feet long, 11 feet wide, and 3½ feet in draft. The sails consist of mizzen, main, and jib, and fishing is done by nets, lines, and small trawls. The most distinctive feature of Hastings luggers aside from their many means of propulsion is their stern form. Originally, they had a large, conventional, transom stern with an outboard rudder. Such a stern eventually was recognized to be a source of difficult handling in a sea and in surf during beach landings, and a modified form was developed. The result is a sort of tucked-up rounded stern which is unique and is apparently an operational improvement. Altogether the Hastings lugger is a most unusual, genuinely indigenous fishing boat.

Another sailing working boat of England survives on the west coast, north of Blackpool on Morecambe Bay, facing the Irish Sea. The prawns taken here are well known, perhaps as tasty as those from Dublin Bay on the opposite shores. Prawning is inshore work that does not involve heavy nets or power blocks on heavy booms. It is done in these protected waters by a fine-looking sailing cutter with a similar rig to that of the oyster boats of Carrick Roadstead, discussed earlier, but a different hull form.

The Morecambe Bay prawner actually has a hull form similar to some of the turn-of-the-century knockabout sloops of the Cape Cod region. The stem has a nicely curved profile, and the stern has a rather long, overhanging counter with the raked rudder hung well below and forward of it. There are some variations in form and dimension, but typical dimensions are 30 feet overall length on a 25-foot waterline, a beam of 9 feet, and a draft of nearly 4 feet at the stern post. These boats are, because of their fine appearance and sailing qualities, often converted to pleasure use. The basic working prawner is decked, with no cabin, but has a large open cockpit abaft the mast. Prawning, like fishing, under sail is becoming a rare thing but there are still a few of these boats working (but with auxiliary motors) from North Wales as far north as Solway Firth.

England and Ireland are separated by more than the Irish Sea. It is difficult, because of England's greater wealth, power, and discernable patronizing attitude, not to lean in the Irish direction. A number of years ago a well-known English authority on ships and boats wrote that the Irish were not a seafaring people and that the only boats they had of value were those built in England and acquired from Cornish, Manx, and Scots fishermen who fished in Irish waters. If this was the situation early in this century when the above opinion was written, I do not find it so today — even the reverse may be true. There are excellent products of native Irish boatbuilding and boat de-

4-23

4-22

signing skills that are commissioned by no less than the Royal National Lifeboat Institution. As an example, Figure 4-22 shows the 70-foot *Grace Patterson Richie* designed by John Tyrrell and Son, yacht and boatbuilders of Arklow, Ireland. While this example may not qualify as an indigenous boat, she is a magnificent vessel and is cited here to dispel any predjudice concerning Irish abilities to build the best seagoing craft.

The Irish tradition of dealing with the cruel seas surrounding her insular realm reaches back to the first days of Christianity in Ireland. As early as the sixth century A.D., there is evidence that Irish Christian monks sailed north to the Faeroe Islands and eventually to Iceland. Like the Scottish and English coasts, the Irish shores also were raided and inhabited from time to time by the Vikings. There were Norse settlements and strongholds at Dublin, Sligo, and other localities in Ireland and it is illogical not to conclude that the boatbuilding skills of these settlers found some root.

On the other hand, the more primitive watercraft of the Celts influenced Irish boatbuilding. Both the Irish and the Welsh can lay claim to surviving remnants of a neolithic culture — the coracle and the curragh.

No one knows, of course, where or how these watercraft were first introduced. It is clear, however, that the primitive ancestors of the early inhabitants of the British Isles first transported themselves to these shores in similar frame-skin boats. The isolated Celtic races, whose energies and

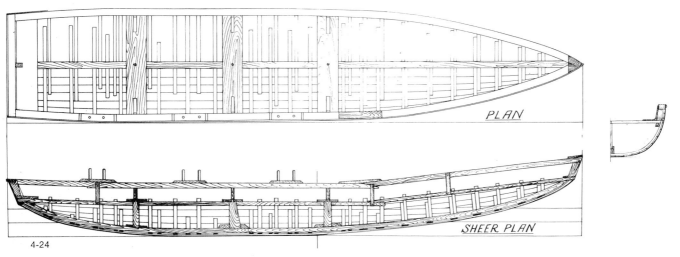

PLAN

SHEER PLAN

4-24

motivations were more agricultural than nautical, found these craft always adequate for their simple requirements on streams, rivers, and even the rocky bays of Galway. They have thus survived for countless centuries with few changes in their original form.

A coracle is a skin or fabric-covered woven wood frame shaped much the same as a half melon. It seldom has a capacity of more than one man and his small burden and is rowed or paddled with a scoop-like paddle. After a log raft and an inflated animal hide, this sort of craft was, no doubt, prehistoric man's first water-born transport. These craft may still be seen occasionally in the vicinity of the River Teifi in Wales. Figure 4-23 shows an example of a Teifi coracle. A very similar type of coracle is indigenous to the River Boyne on Ireland's eastern coast. The Irish generally refer to the fabric-covered frame craft as curraghs.

A slightly more sophisticated curragh is found in Galway, the Aran Islands, and Achill Island on the west coast. This curragh is a step closer to a boat in form as well as construction. The frame is "built" rather than woven (Figure 4-24 shows the construction of an Achill Island Curragh). The island curraghs are larger craft holding three or four men and four to six oars. Their primary advantage is their lightness and transportability. They are truly indigenous craft, and it is a curiosity to find them in such a small land side by side with the finest examples of the modern boatbuilder's art.

One of the best of today's Irish boatbuilders is

4-22 A modern boat of the Royal National Life-Boat Institution. A boat such as this must be capable of operating in any weather of any season. This lifeboat was designed in Ireland and built in Scotland. She is 70 feet long, 17 feet in beam, and 7½ feet in draft.

4-23 The coracle originated long before recorded history. Today's version has a frame of woven, barked tree boughs and a covering of woven, tarred fabric. Originally the covering was the hide of an animal.

4-24 In Ireland a coracle is called a curragh and is more often elongated into a boat form with a more sophisticated frame than the Welsh version. It is still a primitive boat.

4-26

4-25

John Tyrrell and Sons in Arklow. This yard produces boats that are as notable in their fine line and form as those of Scotland. These boats follow the traditional form of the North Sea in their pilot-boat models, but in the fishing craft the basic hull form often favors a transom stern. (See Figure 4-25.)

It is interesting to compare the small lobster-fishing boat of Ireland to the similar fine boats of the opposite side of the Atlantic. Figure 4-26 depicts an Irish lobstering boat that shows considerable similarity to a Maine coast lobsterboat. She is, of course, a heavier boat with a full displacement form and carries less power. On the other hand she is perhaps more comfortable in a heavy chop offshore. Her dimensions are 34 feet by 10 feet, 6 inches, by 4 feet and she is powered by a 36 h.p. Lister diesel which drives her at 7½ knots. Unlike her Scottish relative, she has her wheelhouse forward and is transom sterned. Generally, most of the older boats engaged in the Irish fisheries are double ended with the traditional aft wheelhouse.

A recently built, most sophisticated Irish trawler comparable in size to the Scottish boats is shown in Figure 4-27. The pleasing sweep of sheer and reaching bow of this hull reflects the best of North Sea and old Norse influence, yet her practical lifting transom stern provides a broad platform aft. Her wheelhouse and rig are most modern. She is 65 feet long, 19 feet 3 inches in beam, and 8 feet 6 inches in draft, and is powered by a 240 h.p. Boudouin-type diesel. She is equipped with the

4-25   This modern pilot boat sets the style and standard for many Irish workboats. She was built in Arklow, Ireland.

4-26   An Irish lobsterboat. She is similar in style, though heavier and slower, to the Maine lobsterboat.

4-27   This modern Irish trawler is a large comfortable boat. She is built of African iroko, Irish-grown oak, and teak.

4-27

4-28

latest navigational and electronic aids to fishing as well as auxiliary generating gear and powered deck equipment. Her crew's quarters are centrally heated.

Figure 4-28 shows a typical Irish drift net fisherman tied astern of a pilot boat in the harbor of Tramore. The fishing boat here has a raking stern, the old-style stern inherited from the Scottish luggers of the past century, and an outboard rudder. The pilot boat is a more modern cruiser-stern double ender. Both of these are hull forms, however, that are typical of Scotch, Irish, and North Sea traditions.

As pointed out in the preface, it would be impossible to describe every boat in all of the corners of any geographical region. It is particularly difficult in regions of generally similar cultures, such as the British Isles where the people have been separated politically yet have been united by their industry on the seas. In many respects the trawlers and drifters of Ireland, especially those of Northern Ireland, are quite like the boats of Scotland. Their indigenous quality is created by individual Irish builders and is reflected in the outboard-rudder double enders and transom sterns.

The Irish did not have a great assortment of workboats under sail in the recent past, and few have survived until today. A few sloops, known as Galway hookers, are still at work, however, satisfying the need for basic transportation among the islands of Galway Bay. Used essentially to transport peat fuel to the Aran Islands, the very few barely surviving hookers are over a century old. These boats are poor indeed. They were originally built heavily but economically. They have been patched and marginally maintained through the many years. The character of these boats however, is still clearly unique. They are between 30 and 35 feet in length, carry a gaff main, a staysail, and jib on long bowsprit. The mast and rigging is heavy to the point of being over-scale. The sails are black. The hull form is most unusual in its high freeboard, very full shoulders, tumblehome, and hollow forebody. The hull has a rather straight, flat run in the after body with a full transom stern and outboard rudder. The keel is long and straight, not unlike that of the Danish Skovshoved sildebad (see Chapter 3).

The smallest craft of any locality often retain the most ancient characteristics of the boats that preceded them. This is true of the craft in Scandinavia, the Scottish and North Sea Islands, Portugal, and the Mediterranean, to say nothing of the coracles and curraghs of Wales and Ireland. There is a small skiff of Ireland that is more refined than the curraghs but less sophisticated than the ubiquitous lapstrake rowing boats and dinghies so common in all British and Irish harbors. This fine rowing skiff is found along the Shannon estuary and is about 16 feet in length. It is essentially a flat-bottom boat with the flaring sides of a banks dory, but with four heavy lap planks per side. The stem is gently curved and the narrow transom is roughly wineglass in form. This causes a slight hollow in the counter which is unaccountable in purpose. Because of the resulting curvature in the

4-29

4-28   These two boats in the harbor of Tramore on Ireland's south coast are two different working types. The boat on the left is a modern pilot boat with a trawler stern. The one on the right is a fisherman with a double-ended hull.

4-29   The oldest and one of the only surviving sailing workboats in the British Islands is the Galway hooker of Ireland's west coast. Note the unusual set-back of the laced mainsail from the mast.

4-30   A Shannon River fishing skiff. This is not a boat built to an individual's whim; there are many like it in the area and it is quite different from a common "flattie."

sections, the sawn frames must be curved. It is on the whole a very handsome skiff and is generally rowed by four oars or nowadays more often pushed by a small outboard. Figure 4-30 shows the form and structure of a typical Shannon skiff. It provides native rural water transport and is a fine vehicle for tending nets or handline fishing in western Ireland.

Most of the rowing skiffs and dinghies of Ireland are similar to those of Scotland and England. They are round-bottom boats of conventional lapstrake construction. They have either transom sterns or double ends. Their form is severely conservative and has not changed noticeably for nearly a century and a half. They have become the model for the tenders and lifeboats of larger vessels and are a standard around the world.

It might appear that I have skipped over many important English boat types in my discussion of the British Isles. This is not true. There are simply no great numbers of surviving indigenous English boats. The multiplicity of distinctive types of working sail that operated in English waters three-quarters of a century ago are now extinct. There were Yarmouth luggers, Lowestoft drifters, Mounts Bay drivers, nickies, nobbies, Humber keels, Thames spritsail barges, East Cornish luggers, West Cornish luggers, and many, many others. These boats are all well documented in massive detail in English sources. It is too bad they can only be seen today in books.

4-30

5 / MEDITERRANEAN WORKING CRAFT

THE MEDITERRANEAN, the center of the ancient Western world, has seen the rise and fall of many civilizations. With these civilizations, countless numbers of ships and boats came and went, some triumphantly, some bravely, and some ignominiously. Without a doubt, the earliest sea craft originated at the eastern end of the Mediterranean. The Mediterranean Sea, as well as the Adriatic, Aegean, Ionian, Ligurian, and Tyrrhenian Seas, provided the backdrop for successive island and mainland empires. The Roman Empire flourished and surrounded this sea until it became "Mare Nostrum." Before the Romans, the Greeks dominated the region from Sicily to the Near East. And before the Greeks, the Mycenaeans and the Minoans went forth in capable boats, and so wrote a chapter or two in the book of culture.

On the shores of Lebanon there are still remnants of ancient half-sunken stone breakwaters of the harbors of Phoenician city-states near the sites of Sidon and Tyre. In a place once called Byblos, now Jubayl, there exists, as elsewhere on this coast, a type of remarkably refined inshore beach boat. This boat is natural and graceful with a gentle sheer, well-molded ends, and a proper beam-to-length ratio. Its coefficients of form are modern in the most approved sense, and yet it is so timeless that its origin cannot be estimated. It is possible to say that this beach boat could well be the model, indeed the pattern, that is the basis for all Mediterranean beach boats. The beach and harbor boats so prevalent throughout this whole great sea have a common look with, of course, many regional variants. This boat seems to be a recognizable root, as basic to boat design perhaps as Latin and Greek are to modern languages.

The Lebanese beach boat is a smoothly planked, typically Mediterranean double-ender with a rising stem post. Its distinguishing feature, and also the characteristic that reinforces my belief in its originality, is its restrained design. Its sheer line, for example, is more gently curved than that of most other Mediterranean beach boats; the stem post does not rise quite as high; and the hull is also of less depth. These are all features that when first devised were perhaps innovations. Essentially this boat has a clean canoe-shaped body with no abrupt changes in curvature, yet with sufficient curvature to have a natural hollow in the bow without a shoulder. The construction is on the heavy side, with sawn frames, carvel planking and often a heavier rub-rail plank below the sheer plank. The boat is from 16 to 20 feet in length, and is generally powered with a small one-cylinder engine. In the past, it was rowed, or sailed with a short lateen sail. It is a graceful boat whose ancestry is lost somewhere in the mists of perhaps ten centuries past — or even more.

The oldest civilizations on the Mediterranean shores were those of the people of the Nile. While the Egyptians have never been a seapower, they have been water oriented. Nearly the total population is confined to the fertile strip of land bordering the edge of the Nile and its estuary. The earliest inhabitants here were probably the first to

5-1

exploit effectively boats of any sort. The primitive watercraft still used on the Nile are of interest primarily because of the origin of their ancient sails. The sail form still used here, like the Lebanese boat described previously, is probably an original: the lateen sail was first evident on the Nile. The lateen is now a popular and widely adapted rig. In Egypt, it retains its original form — a graceful, triangular fore-and-aft sail with a towering yard peaked high above the masthead.

Long ago on the upper reaches of the Nile, sails had always been "square" or spread on yards. As shown in the earliest dynastic reliefs, the yards were tilted upward to reach for breezes above the trees or sandy cliffs. The part of the sail in the downward position was in the way and of little use, and so it was trimmed back. This sail can still be seen today above the second cataract of the Nile on a boat type called a nugger. This rig is known as the nugger lug.

On the lower Nile some working boats today are notable for the great spread of their ancient triangular sails. In all of the regions where the lateen is still in any use — in Portugal, most Mediterranean regions, the Black Sea, the Red Sea, and the Persian Gulf, as far east as India and south to the African coast — no sailors can equal the Arabs of the Nile in maneuvering boats equipped with this rig. The boats using these great sails are not noted for their shape, structure, or for anything else except their surprising performance beneath their bulging triangular canopy. This lower Nile boat type is known generally as a gaias-

sa. It is sometimes two masted, but more often nowadays it has a single, forward-raking mast carrying the long lateen yard. This yard, often 80 feet or more in length, is made up of sections, overlapped and lashed crudely together, a universal practice with lateens. The yard is not generally lowered when the sail is shortened or furled, but the crew goes aloft, straddling the yard as if it were a sloping tree trunk.

The gaiassa's hull is a flat, broad, barge-form with a swept-up spoon-like bow for keeping the cargo dry, as the bow wave piles up when the boat is running against the river chop. This bow, with its exaggerated rise, is perhaps the last remnant of any likeness to the magnificent high-ended river boats that sailed the Nile four thousand or more years ago.

To the westerner, the method of sailing a gaiassa is unusual. When sailing on the wind, the yard carries the sail to windward of the weather rigging. As with the older lateens it is customary to wear around because the yard is above and outside the shrouds and rigging. When wearing, the gaiassa's yard is hauled around aft of the mast so that the yard is always on the windward side of the mast. When sailing free or off the wind, the tack ropes on the lower end of the yard are slacked off and the sail forms a lifting air foil overhead, carrying the craft gracefully along. The sailor of a gaiassa could probably not sail any other type of sailing craft, even if it were lateen rigged, but then no other sailor could possibly manage a gaiassa.

There were a number of small lateen-rigged

5-2

5-1 Before the Arab-Israeli wars, there were many varied types of boats working at the Mediterranean entrance to the Suez Canal. This stone lighter with a settee rig, a variation of the lateen rig, is representative of a mixture of Eastern and Mediterranean cultures.

5-2 Three two-masted gaiassas, heavily laden, sailing downwind on the Nile. Still taking advantage of the nearly constant upstream wind as all Egyptian boats have for over 5,000 years, these boats could very well be the direct descendants of the very first boats to sail.

5-3 Model of a two-masted gaiassa. Note the large rudder, swept-up bow, and three-piece, lashed main yard.

harbor and delta craft on the coast from Port Said to Alexandria before the Arab-Israeli wars. These boats have suffered, as did the boats of the Brittany coast during World Wars I and II, from the ravages of war and the interruption of peaceful commerce. It is unlikely that these craft will be replaced.

The Bronze Age trade routes, carrying the first sea commerce, led first to the Levant coast (modern Lebanon, Israel, and Syria). The Egyptians, always in search of timber, found the cedars of the Levant most useful and valuable. But in the years of the third millennium B.C., another people were trading and sailing in superior boats. The Egyptians called this new race of sailors simply the "People of the Sea." We know them as the Minoans. Their homeland was Crete and the Aegean Islands, and they began a long line of sea-oriented people. Of their boats we know relatively little, except what we can deduce from their voyages and trade routes. The Minoans completely dominated the trade routes and harbors of the eastern and central Mediterranean. Their boats were superior, and they were more skilled navigators than any of their contemporaries. The legacy of their boats and their sea knowledge is not noticeable today, perhaps because their contributions were so basic. The Minoan boatwrights were the first to conceive a boat with a frame structure. Their boats had keels, stem and stern posts, and transverse frames. This ancient concept is today

5-3

the universal practice in the structure of both small boats and large ships, and has been constantly in use for these thousands of years since the Aegean builders first devised it.* But there are few workboats in the Aegean today that reflect the older culture.

Boats are produced, however, in a style indigenous to the eastern Mediterranean, and they are found particularly in the Aegean and on the Turkish littoral. There is first, a type of trading schooner frequently of Greek origin to be seen among the islands and in the small harbors of the eastern coast. Most of these schooners carry a conventional gaff rig nowadays, instead of the formerly popular sprit or lug-sail rig. The masts are comparatively short with no topsails ("bald headed" as the rig was referred to by American sailors a century ago.) The hulls are deep and full, of heavy displacement, but with a nice sheer line culminating forward in a rising, flaring bow. The stem form is a fairly common Mediterranean profile, and Americans would describe it as a "clipper" bow. It is, however, a far older and more subtle form than the bow form of the American nineteenth century clipper. It most surely evolved from the rakish stems of the old Turkish and Saracen galleys which were so impressively predominant as warcraft centuries ago. This stem profile can be seen on other Mediterranean craft, described later.

There seem to be no rigorous rules surrounding the proportions or form of the eastern Mediterranean trading schooners. The individuality of their builders is freely expressed. These vessels

5-4

*The only departure from this basic structure is the recent fabrication of small hulls in molded fiberglass-reinforced plastic and ferro-cement.

5-5

may have broad transoms carrying the heavy rudder stock outboard or they may have a more graceful rounded or eliptical stern on a short counter overhang. The gunwales are deep and heavily built, and they have wide decks broken by but one heavily framed hatch, a companionway, and a small deckhouse. The boats vary between 50 and 75 feet in length. The style and color are always unmistakably eastern Mediterranean.

The eastern Mediterranean hull, with its variable rig, overhanging stem, and either transom or short counter stern, is seemingly increasing in popularity in the smaller sizes, particularly the boats of approximately 30 feet in length. These smaller boats among the Aegean islands generally have a short rig with a single mast. They depend primarily on a one-cylinder diesel of large displacement. The sail may be a lateen, but usually it is a lugsail or conventional low-cut gaff sail. The most notable characteristic of these boats — they seem to have fallen into a recognizable style — is the attention that the builder pays to producing a nicely formed hull. These boats are purely Greek and can be seen in the crowded harbor of Piraeus or in any of the small island harbors between Hydra and Rhodes. They are used for inter-island transport, fishing, or more frequently these days, since the discovery of the Greek islands by tourists, as charter boats (together with an assortment of other nondescript types). They have been erroneously called caiques, and have been imported to or duplicated in Florida by Greek sponge fishermen. Although it is not the typical sponge boat

used in Tarpon Springs, Florida, the type is occasionally seen there. Figure 5-4 shows one of these boats in a builder's yard just after completion of the hull. The excellent workmanship is clearly evident in this well-modeled 30-footer. Note the typical Mediterranean bow bitheads extending from the bow rail. These bitheads are standard in all types of Mediterranean boats, both eastern and western. Identical ones were used on the ships and boats of ancient Rome.

A common boat of the Aegean, yet one that evades categorization, is also an island trading boat. It is similar in size to the schooner type described previously. It is the nearest contemporary relative, sometimes an actual conversion, of the Greek and Turkish sailing coasters so common in the nineteenth century. These were great sprit or lug-rigged craft of deep sheer with low waists protected by built-up sheer strakes added as waist rails. (These are the modern version of the old woven fabric waist cloth that dates back to the second millennium B.C. and earlier.) The termination of this sheer planking forward produces a unique bow and stem form that identifies the boat as Greek.

Among the small ports of the Levant coast and in the Aegean Sea, there are still cargo-carrying boats with an unusual assortment of rigs. Some of these are related to the old polacres or Mediterranean square-riggers with pole masts. These boats are sometimes conventionally square-rigged brigs or brigantines with single pole masts 60 to 80 feet in height, generally exhibiting the steep

sheer of Mediterranean boats, or they can be stub
by-masted schooners or large ketches with one la
teen and one gaff-headed sail and perhaps a squar
yard on the main. Such odd craft are difficult t
classify, because they are the result of individua
experimentation together with some ancestral o
ancient influences. They are interesting to stud
individually, but they cannot be identified as in
digenous types. They are mentioned here only t
note their presence and to isolate them from mor
important craft.

Smaller but very common Greek fishing type
are found in many individual variations through
out the Aegean area. They are typical of the Gree
islands. (See Figures 5-6 and 5-8.) The boats hav
a deep sheer with rising ends, often have a spra
curtain along the waist (an Aegean usage that ca
be observed on a Greek vase painting of a ship in
the fourth century B.C.), and have a stem pos
that extends approximately nine to ten inche
above the forward deck. This stem post frequent
ly has a distinctive semicircular cutout carved in
the after edge. The mast is comparatively shor
and the loose-footed sail is for steadying and ca
be used for auxiliary drive. These boats are gen
erally double enders but are now frequently buil
with a broad wineglass transom popular among
Aegean builders. It is interesting that the double
ended form used here is often hollow with flarin
after sections. Such a stern can be seen in the lit
tle Aegean sponge-fishing boat of Figure 5-7.

The sponge-diving industry in the Aegean ha
suffered in recent years because the local spong

5-6 A double-ended Aegean fishing boat. Note the built-up sheer strake and the fabric spray shield.

5-7 This sponger is typical of all of the smaller boats of the Aegean. This type is identified primarily by the shape of its raised stem. This broad stem is always carved in profile with a semicircular cutout in the after edge.

5-8 A double-ended Aegean fishing boat. Note the tiller curving down from the high rudder head.

5-7

5-8

127

5-9   *A small Greek beach boat used for fishing. This type is indigenous to the Gulf of Corinth and sails with a light sprit rig. Because it does not have a high stem, this boat is unique. It is a fine-lined double ender with a raking stem and stern.*

5-10   *The hull lines profile of a balikci, a comparatively recent development in Black Sea and Bosphorous fishing craft. This boat, however, is an extension of older traditions that have for centuries characterized Saracen boats.*

5-9

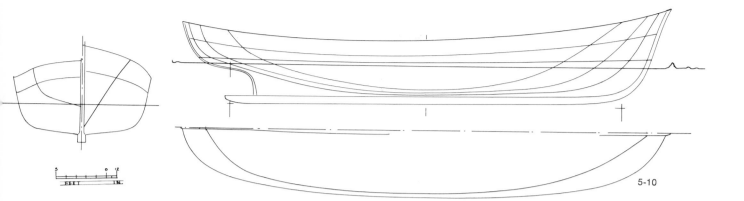

5-10

beds have been depleted. The Greek boats now sail to the grounds off the African shore for sponges. Poor local fishing has had an adverse effect on the old boats previously used in sponging that were similar to but larger than those existing now. Some of these older types were prevalent in Tarpon Springs, Florida.

The Greeks have an instinctive feeling for line and form, which is their inheritance, and it is so apparent in all of their boats. The structure and form of the boats built, owned, and sailed by Greeks are the best and most sea-kindly in the whole Mediterranean. It probably has always been so.

Fishing craft and trading boats used beyond the Dardanelles in Turkish waters have successfully survived the transition from sail to power. In the process the Turks have retained and improved the strong regional character of their boats.

The boats of Turkey retain the quality of structure that began with the Ottoman empire when expense was of very little consequence and the Sultans imported the best craftsmen from wherever they were to be found. It was in the building of the Moslem galleys that the tradition of Turkish excellence in boat carpentry began. That the skills of the past have been passed on from generation to generation is obvious in the present-day boats active as fishing craft and coastal traders out of Istanbul and the Black Sea.

The most typical and well-defined Turkish boats are found in and around Istanbul and the Sea of Marmara. They are either coastal carrier

boats or fishing craft, mostly engine-powered today but some with short auxiliary sailing rigs. Of the fishing types, the most notable is a seiner of the Istanbul locality known as a balikci. Although this boat type is a recent development of perhaps only the last 50 years, it has a regional character strong enough to be considered indigenous. This type is generally from 45 to 50 feet in length, and its form is characterized by a graceful sheer, fine entrance, powerful bows, and a trawler-type overhanging stern. The keel is straight with a slight drag, and its draft of about 5.5 feet allows fairly easy beaching when necessary. The general hull shape and structure is in the finest tradition of low-powered sea-kindly forms. (See Figure 5-10.) These boats have been studied extensively in towing tank programs sponsored by the Food and Agriculture Organization under the direction of Professor Ata Nutku of the Technical University in Istanbul. The builders have been most responsive subsequently to further development and improvement of the type. These balikci are capable boats in the most modern sense. Their structure is, however, of the most conservative sort with closely spaced sawn frames together with heavy keels and keelsons. The planking is carvel with deep gunwales and heavy rail caps.

An older type of craft on this northern Turkish shore is a freight carrier called a tchektirme. These boats, still abundant, were developed from older sailing craft once fitted with a large triangular sail. The identifying character of a tchektirme is its deep, exaggerated sheer line. This sheer line

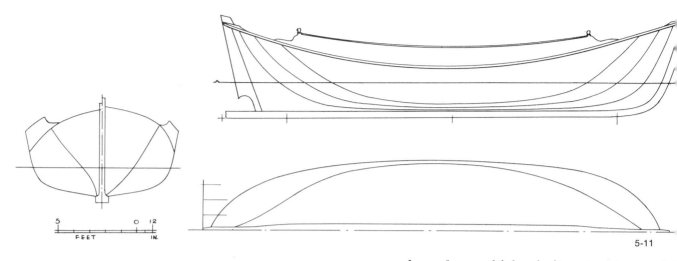

5-11

sweeps down from a high scimitar stem to a waist that, when loaded, may be at or below the water-line, and then sweeps aft to a high stern post. Above the guard rail of the apparent sheer line, however, is a higher bulwark. This feature is reminiscent of the classic Aegean boats, which required a wash or spray rail to protect the amidships area. This higher bulwark curves up from the upper guard rail abaft the bow chocks (See Figure 5-12.) and again back down to the after rail line. The modified lines drawing of a small but typical tchektirme shown in Figure 5-11 indicates the classic profile of this type. It is notable that the deck line is always flatter than the apparent sheer line in these boats. Tchektirmes vary in size from small, almost miniature craft of less than 30 feet, to quite large boats, sometimes as much as 80 feet in length.

Very seldom are contemporary tchektirmes seen under sail. However, when they do carry auxiliary sail, the rig consists of a short lug mainsail or triangular sail with a long foot and a conventional jib or foresail rigged to a housing bowsprit.

The taka is perhaps less numerous but no less distinctive in style than the tchektirme. Takas are distinguished first by the unusual profile of their upper stem. This distinctive shape has been unflatteringly, but very descriptively, called a "chicken beak" stem. (See Figure 5-14.) The sheer line of a taka is very extreme and similar to the tchektirme's. The upper bulwark is also characteristic of the tchektirme, but it extends all the way to the stern in a taka. The taka's stern form is also

5-12

130

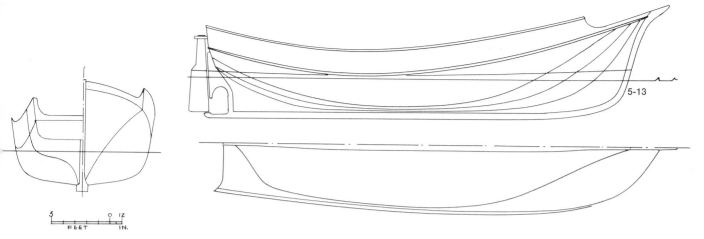

5-13

5-14

distinctive, being a square transom stern formed quite high on the stern post. The stern post is frequently set partially outside the transom, and the rudder is hung conventionally outboard with the curved tiller projecting through the stern. (See Figure 5-13.)

Takas have generally well-proportioned hulls aside from their stubby-looking after end which results in less than a clean, flat run. The basic taka may range in size from a boat of about 18 feet up to a sizable coaster of 60 feet carrying perhaps 250 tons deadweight.

It is most evident that in Turkey the type of boat developed is generally not dictated by a single employment. Very seldom is it possible to observe indigenous boats whose distinctive forms and character are the result of the specific requirements of a fishing technique. The most usual circumstance is that a boat type must be adaptable to several modes of employment to survive successfully. This general truth is well illustrated throughout the Mediterranean as well as at its eastern end. The takas and tchektirmes are built in all sizes and are employed as seiners, handliners, coastal carriers, traders, or in whatever water transport suits the owner or which he finds immediately most profitable.

In my discussion of Aegean boats a caique was mentioned. While this term may often be used to describe Aegean craft, it is more properly applied to a specific small rowing craft in Istanbul and the Sea of Marmara. This boat is undoubtedly a decendent of a very elegant boat. The Sultans

5-11   The hull lines of a small tchektirme. The tchektirme is built in various sizes from less than 30 feet to more than 80 feet in length.

5-12   The Turkish tchektirme is certainly the most common trading boat in the Bosporus and the Black Sea. It is also seen in the eastern Mediterranean, and its relation to the Greek island traders is apparent in the bows and the waist boards along the sides. Since World War II, the tchektirmes have all gradually been converted to power; formerly they carried a two-masted lug rig.

5-13   The lines of a taka in this modified profile show the curious features of this traditional Turkish boat. Note the high quarter rail and outboard rudder head.

5-14   The taka is a very short-ended boat distinguished by its unique false stem extension. The boat is stubby and flat floored, and has a high, flaring bow — an inefficient but curiously attractive hull form.

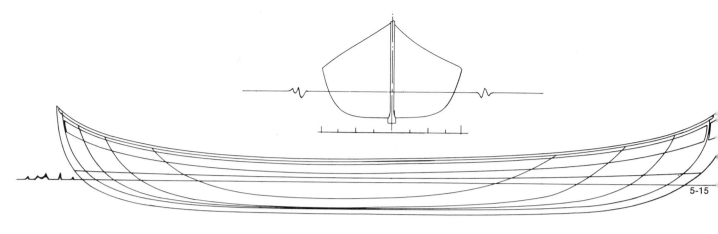

5-15

of three to four centuries ago were transported with great pomp in a multi-oared, high-ended, decorated boat called a caique or kayik in Turkish.

Today the surviving kayik is a very graceful double ender whose simplified profile lines are shown in Figure 5-15. The boat has a canoe-like profile, but is quite broad of beam; the beam and fullness is carried well aft where the greater weight is carried. This boat type is still colorfully decorated and embellished with carving and has gracefully formed ends. Its name, however, like the names of many fine and functional artifacts and devices of men, has become popularized and extended to other like objects of lesser quality. So today we are not quite sure what a caique is when someone uses the name.

On the old trade route from the Aegean around Peloponnesus through the Ionian Sea and up the Adriatic there is a timeless quality to the sea. With only a little imagination one sees misty images of ancient ships against the blue haze of the mountainous shore. Long after the Minoan traders, Greek merchant ships, and the Roman triremes disappeared, this route led to the powerful Venetian state. The elaborate war galleys of Venice ventured forth from this seaway with flashing oars to diminish the power of the Ottoman navies. This heart of the Mediterranean today brings to mind many memories of world sea power, wealth, commerce, and a great progression of rational shipbuilding. Today's boats in this area are but a poor and shabby reflection of such past glory. There are several types whose operation

and origin identifies them with this region, b[ut] they are only the remnants of a recent coastwi[se] commerce under sail. It is still possible to e[n]counter a few of these craft under sail, but [it] is a rare encounter. Most hulls are converted [to] mechanical power with auxiliary sail.

In the southern end of the Adriatic near th[e] Ionian Sea, where Italy is nearest to Greec[e,] the boats observed are much like those to b[e] found in the Aegean and about the Greek ha[r]bors. But farther into the Adriatic there is a notic[e]able change in character. The most predominan[t] boat, one that originated in the region of Ancon[a] a century or more ago, is a very full and blu[nt] coasting vessel called a trabaccolo. This boat ha[s] two masts carrying two lugsails, and it has a larg[e] jib set flying on a steeply raked bowsprit. It has [a] colorful, striped, double-ended hull and a ta[ll] rudder. The boat's most distinctive feature is th[e] fullness of its ends, particularly its bows, whic[h] terminate in a backward-raking stem. It has an u[n]gainly round-bilge hull with shallow flat section[s.] Trabaccolos are usually 50 to 70 feet long, but ar[e] sometimes found in smaller sizes around 40 fee[t] with a single-masted lug rig.

A typical, ancient decoration found on sma[ll] indigenous craft in almost all parts of the worl[d] is the "oculus." This often painted, sometime[s] carved, eye in the bows of boats was first used i[n] the eastern Mediterranean. It was common as ea[r]ly as the middle of the first millennium, B.C., an[d] is evident on pottery decorations showing Gree[k] ships of this time. On the trabaccolo, the ocul[us]

5-15 The long, graceful canoe-like hull lines of a caique. The Turkish caique is actually the one genuine caique of several misnamed types. It is used in contemporary Turkish fisheries as a net-handling boat and fishes in conjunction with the balikci.

5-16 The classic, centuries-old trabaccolo of the Adriatic is best illustrated by this native model. Note the full lug rig and housing bowsprit with headsail. These boats are still occasionally seen under this rig, but most often they have a cut-down mast and are diesel powered. The boats are distinguished by their high, bluff, swept-up bows and heavy, carved oculus.

5-17 A well-worn trabaccolo with a shortened rig.

5-16

5-17

5-18 Three double-ended fishing luggers typical of the Adriatic. Similar to the trabaccolo in rig, they have more practical sailing hulls with finer lines.

5-19 The small craft of the Adriatic, as elsewhere, reflect much of the character of their larger contemporaries. The extended side washboards are influences of boats from the Aegean and Ionian Seas.

5-20 The trabaccolos of more than a century and a half ago, as illustrated by Antoine Roux, are similar to the craft in Figure 5-18. The rig and general character have hardly changed.

5-18

5-19

serves as a functional part of the boat as well. It is a carving that surrounds the hawse hole in both sides of the bow, such as in Figure 5-16.

The trabaccolo is a trading boat that is often found outside of the Adriatic sailing into Malta, Sicily, or the eastern ports. However, its own locale is the upper Adriatic near Venice and Ancona. It is unmistakable with its colorful, full-ended hull and high bows pushing a white bow wave down the Adriatic.

An Adriatic lugger more trim in line and rig than the trabaccolo is more frequently encountered today. This traditional fishing lugger of the upper Adriatic is 45 to 50 feet long, though sometimes larger, with a lively but not excessive sheer. It has two masts; the forward one is slightly taller and carries the larger sail. These boats are typical of the Adriatic with their high narrow rudders, broad rudder heads, deep gunwales, and boomed lugsails of the eastern Mediterranean. Like the larger trabaccolos, they are planked and framed in oak with decks of pine, but they are proportionately deeper, not as beamy, and have a much finer entrance and run.

It is curious that this lugger is very much the same boat as that illustrated by the great marine artist, Antoine Roux, in 1816 which he identifies as "Trabacolo" (see Figure 5-20). It is possible that the present-day concept of a trabaccolo has a more recent origin, or, on the other hand, that Monsieur Roux, who did most of his work in Marseille, was relying on a general Italian identification. It is a reasonable speculation, in any case,

5-20

5-21

5-21 The bragozzo of Venice is the traditional sailing barge of the lagoons of the North Adriatic. It is a hard-working, ungainly craft.

5-22 A Venetian gondola. All gondoliers stand on the port side as they row. The single oar is for both rowing and steering.

5-23 Though gondolas are similar in style and form, they differ in decoration. Notice the forward deck ornamentation on these two gondolas — one plain and one fancy.

5-24 The bow ornament of two gondolas.

that the handsome eighteenth century lugger, as painted by Roux, was the ancestor of these later Adriatic luggers. It should also be pointed out that the larger, fuller, bluff-bowed trabaccolo is a trading vessel carrying lumber and stone about the coastal ports while the smaller version is a fishing boat. There is often such a distinction in a basic type of workboat, but seldom is there so great a difference in form.

In the lagoons of Venice there still may be seen an occassional sailing barge called a bragozzo, which when under sail is distinctive in its sail decoration. It has a large main lugsail and a very small one on a short mast well forward, with no other headsail. The bragozzo is a clumsy flat-bottomed barge-like vessel. (See Figure 5-21.)

In any discussion such as this of indigenous watercraft, it would be a slight to the Venetians to ignore the most familiar of all indigenous boats. The gondola of Venice is at once a taxi, a ferry, a truck, and a family vehicle, and varies in appearance from humble to luxurious. As of this writing its future is threatened, as it has been on other occassions. However, this current threat may be of more serious consequence. The ancient craft of gondola building is dying for want of young apprentices. None of these graceful, unique, beautifully built little canoe-like hulls are of recent construction. Not too long ago there were in Venice 10,000 of these boats; only a few hundred remain today.

The Venetian gondola is a very special watercraft whose qualities and employment are in most

respects not comparable to the other boats discussed in this book. (See Figures 5-22, 5-23, and 5-24.) It is, however, nothing if not indigenous to its locale. It is a craft rigorously bound by tradition. It has had no major changes in its design and styling perhaps for 500 years. Its light canoe-like hull may vary in length from 30 to 50 feet, though the standard gondola of today is 36 feet. Always painted black, its graceful hull is sheathed with several strakes of thin planking over approximately 40 delicately sawn frames. It is open for two thirds of its length, but there is a deck aft of its canopy that forms a platform for the gondolier and his single sweep. The starboard side of the boat is eight inches shorter than the port side to offset the drag of the oar. The gondolier's oar-sweep works in a raised carved oarlock on the starboard side allowing him to row and steer simultaneously from his standing position to port. The ends rise steeply, with the stem carrying the traditional gondola-identifying decoration, which consists of a number of spiked projections turned forward, reminiscent of old galley rams, and one turned aft. The graceful stern is often unnoticed because it is overshadowed by the ostentatious bow. The gondola is simply the basic unit or common denominator of transportation in Venice, where the waters once swarmed with glittering varieties of more elaborate, oared, galley-like transports.

Before this discussion of watercraft in the Adriatic is ended, it should be re-emphasized that the existing craft today are reflections and remnants of a comparatively recent domination of a great

5-22

5-23

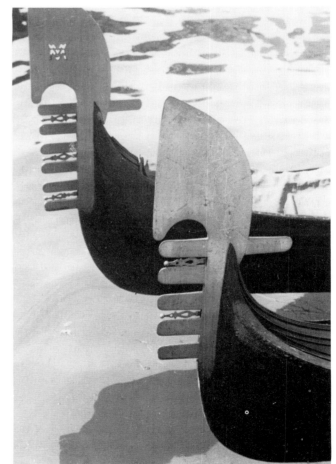

5-24

5-25

variety of sailing craft. This is true not only of the Adriatic but also of the entire eastern Mediterranean. There was a marked similarity in all these sailing workboats with their sweeping, often exaggerated sheer lines and high ends, their weather canvas or raised bulwarks protecting the amidships waists, the high aspect rudders, and, most of all, the popular balanced lugsail rig.

This lugsail, which carries a boom on its foot unlike the northern lug of the British and French coasts, is similar and, some say, related to the oriental version of the lug rig. It is my belief that this rig evolved as a result of a gradual development of the lateen rig — a rig that is indigenous to the eastern Mediterranean. There is no objective evidence that is specific enough to indicate the real origin of either the lug rig or the lateen. The classic Greek and subsequent Roman sail of the pre-Christian era was the basic square sail and, in some occasional instances, a sprit sail, apparently on small craft. Sometime, in the years that followed, the lateen and lugsails appeared. They could most logically have originated very simply by experimentation and adaptation of the square sail to other than downwind sailing, as on the Nile. Such experimentation would most likely take place in the smaller craft, which were undermanned and could not conveniently rely on oars. Most large vessels, except for the slow and independent traders, were basically galleys or oar-powered boats, because the Mediterranean is a sea of light and unreliable winds, varied by sudden and violent weather in the winter months. It is not

a sea to encourage development of large, complex sailing rigs. The lugsail was a natural development and is still the basic sail of the Aegean and Adriatic where working sail is used, even as an auxiliary. In the western Mediterranean there is no compromise with the lateen.

The geographical center of the Middle Sea is very close to the islands of Malta, and it is in this British bastion that there is to be found a style of watercraft combining the nautical practices and heritages of the East and West. There are two distinctive types of craft still evident and indigenous to Malta. One is a combination fishing and transport boat, while the other is essentially for harbor transport and is only propelled by a single oarsman.

This latter harbor boat, the Maltese dghaisa used still in Grand Harbor, Malta, is not unrelated in character and utility to the Venetian gondola. In structure and appearance, however, there is a difference. (See Figure 5-25.) The dghaisa (sometimes called draissa) is a much heavier, fuller boat than the gondola. The oarsman stands well amidships and facing forward and with crossed oar looms propels the boat with short even strokes. Surrounding the central open area of this boat there is a raised rail and seats along the side for passengers. There is often a higher carved backrest in the after end. The stem and stern posts are high, nearly vertical, but with a slight inward rake and with the greatest width at the top. The

5-25 *The Maltese dghaisa, like the Venetian gondola, is an all-purpose harbor craft. The differences in configuration, however, are as readily apparent as the similarities. The high ends of the Maltese boat are like great scimitars. The boatman stands and rows facing forward with crossed oar looms. This dghaisa has an auxiliary outboard motor.*

5-26 *The Maltese dghaisa-tal-pass is a colorful inter-island carrier and harbor boat. Though each boat is decorated differently, they all share certain features. For example, there is always on each bow a small but distinctive oculus. The traditional wash rail is removable in*

sections, a practice which began at least a century and a half ago from the evidence in Antoine Roux's record of these boats. The distinctive shape of this boat is its most immediate identification. It has a steep forward sheer and high, broad extended stem; it is somewhat related to the boats of the Adriatic.

5-27 *This painting by Antoine Roux in 1826 shows a taffarel, the graceful ancestor of today's Maltese boats. She carries a sprit rig here, which several centuries ago was the popular sail of boats in the Ionian and Aegean Seas. Note the removable waist panels, common today, for convenience in rowing.*

5-26

5-27

stem post is nicely scimitar-shaped in the Turkish fashion, while the stern post is cut off horizontally. The boats are generally from 20 to 25 feet long with a beam of about six feet. They are nicely cared for, generally painted brightly with a white waterline boot-top and natural varnished sheer plank and end posts.

For transport between the islands, particularly between Malta and Gozo, and sometimes for fishing, there is a larger more capable boat. This boat, called by the more awkward title dghaisa-tal-pass, is quite shapely and is heavily constructed in the manner of all Mediterranean beach boats. (See Figure 5-26.) This craft, also sometimes called a taffarel, is distinctive with an upswept bow and high stem characteristic of Malta. It has a deep waist with high protective gunwale in the fashion of the Turkish and Aegean boats. This gunwale, however, is arranged in removable flat panels, perhaps to accommodate oars or for more convenient loading in harbor. On the forward rail there are king posts, which rise above the rail panels and provide a base of attachment for them. These contemporary boats are all motor-powered today but formerly carried a sprit rig and long bowsprit, as can be seen in a most charming water color by the celebrated French artist Antoine Roux in 1826 (see Figure 5-27). Their hulls have lost none of their color or charm and are brightly painted in several colors, often in blues that match the sea with yellow and red trim. The oculus in the bows of the dghaisa-tal-pass is ever-present.

The largest typically Maltese workboat is the

5-28

present-day version of the old speronara. This boat today is very like the dghaisa-tal-pass but is larger, heavier, and carries an auxiliary sail, although it is basically a powered craft. The sail is a high-peaked lateen or a settee on a short mast. The hull is beamy, about 14 feet wide to an overall length of 45 feet, with fine ends. It has the characteristic Maltese upswept bow with a high stem forward, rail posts, and a paneled gunwale washrail. The rudder is deep, has a high aspect ratio, and rises slightly above the stern post aft. This boat is a handsome, capable sea boat in the best tradition of the Mediterranean. The Maltese can be justly proud of all their well-kept indigenous boats, but mostly of this lateener.

Although Malta is at the center of the Mediterranean and has been for centuries a military bastion commanding the comings and goings of commerce between the East and West, it has not been a site for the development of a separate culture. But just to the north of Malta is the historic land of Sicily—a large, fertile, and beautiful island. The fine arts to be found in Sicily, the great Greek temples with handsome columns still standing, the decorative arts of the people reflecting Norman establishments, the Byzantine architecture and mosaics, and the medieval cloisters and baroque cathedrals all testify that here the West and Near East fell in together. The situation suggests that whatever indigenous watercraft are built and used here might also show some evidence of a blending of such mixed cultures. Unfortunately, there is little left but traces.

In Sicily, the indigenous horse- and donkey-drawn carts are colorfully decorated with scenes of Sicilian history, much of it with medieval themes. These decorations are occasionally carried over to small fishing boats and harbor craft (see Figure 5-28). But the more basic features of Sicilian boats are found in their shape and construction. One's very first impression is that they are heavy and rugged; their stem and stern posts are similar to Maltese boats, but their hull shape is more like western Mediterranean craft. Figure 5-29 is a sketch made in Palermo harbor of a typical shapely but shabby little harbor boat about 18 feet long.

The larger fishing boats which engage in a community endeavor common among Sicilian fishermen called trap net fishing are similar in general construction to the harbor boat. They are not as deep in hull, however, and are narrower and flatter of sheer in proportion. The dimensions of an average trap net boat are 32 feet overall, 30 feet waterline, 8½ feet beam, and 1½ feet draft (light). As is evident from the profile in Figure 5-30 these boats carry a large raking lateen sail and a deep rudder. They are fitted also for from six to eight oars. These lateen-rigged boats work in conjunction with a larger barge-like craft of 55 feet or so in length, which carries and works the heavy nets. Much of the fishing in Sicily is carried on this way.

A Sicilian boat that is well known because of its

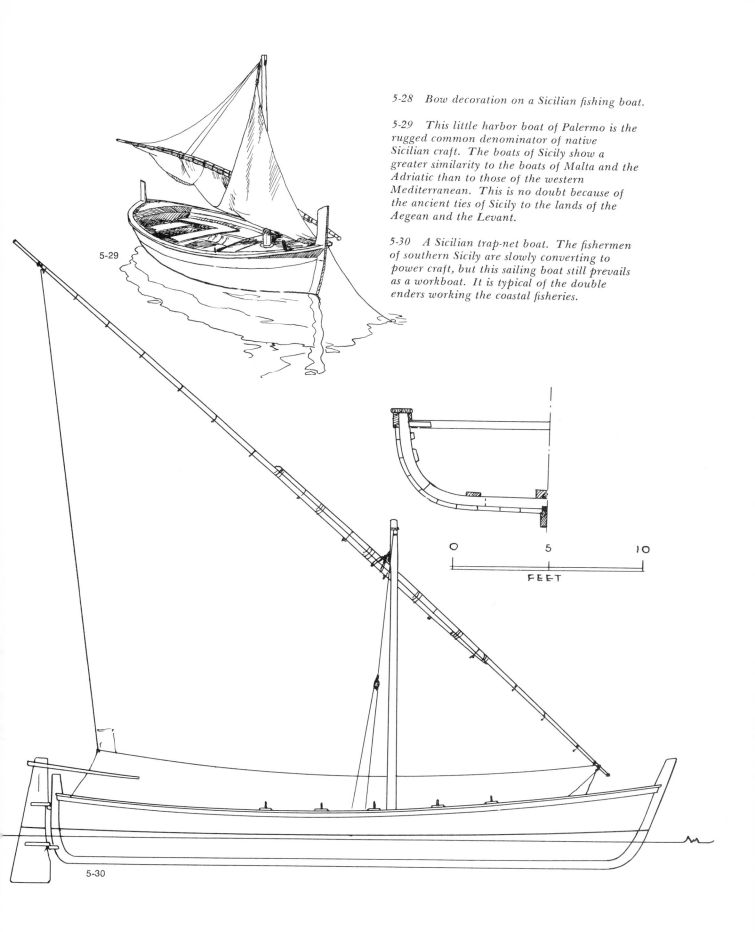

5-28 *Bow decoration on a Sicilian fishing boat.*

5-29 *This little harbor boat of Palermo is the rugged common denominator of native Sicilian craft. The boats of Sicily show a greater similarity to the boats of Malta and the Adriatic than to those of the western Mediterranean. This is no doubt because of the ancient ties of Sicily to the lands of the Aegean and the Levant.*

5-30 *A Sicilian trap-net boat. The fishermen of southern Sicily are slowly converting to power craft, but this sailing boat still prevails as a workboat. It is typical of the double enders working the coastal fisheries.*

5-29

0   5   10

FEET

5-30

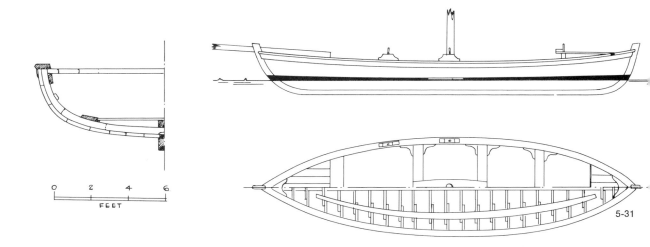

5-31

unique appearance, which evolved from its special employment as a harpoon boat, is the swordfishing craft working in the Straits of Messina. This swordfish catcher when working is rigged with a long bowsprit-like pulpit platform, which is approximately as long as or slightly longer than the boat itself. This long pulpit is supported by a tall mast. The hull of this boat is shown in the profile sketch in Figure 5-31. This small swordfish boat is a shapely double ender not too unlike an old American whale boat. It is about 20 feet in length on a beam of 6 feet with a 2 foot depth from gunwale to keel. It is almost completely open, with three thwarts and short decks forward and aft. It has short projecting stem and stern posts and a gentle, natural sheer, but these features are more restrained in this Sicilian boat than in most other Mediterranean boats.

In recent years a new and larger type of harpoon boat has been introduced to Sicily. The larger boat is still changing and developing, but its features, designed to improve fishing techniques, comprise a longer pulpit platform which, added to the increased size of the boat, allows the harpooner to be over the fish when the stern of the boat is 80 to 100 feet away (see Figure 5-32). This distance makes motor power possible. By rigging-in the pulpit platform this larger boat is capable of hunting swordfish farther at sea. The smaller boat will no doubt continue to be used and, while fishing less efficiently, will remain unimproved and unchanged. Hopefully it will not die out. Swordfishing is a seasonal operation and the boats must

remain versatile for other modes of fishing.

While the western shores of Italy are not particularly distinguished for their characteristic water craft today, the colorful boats which were there in abundance a century or more ago may still be seen in Sardinia. Many of these Sardinian craft still carry sail (the pure lateen) and are typical of larger craft formerly used in the Ligurian and Tyrrhenian Seas.

Of the larger working craft, an occasional vessel remains from the recently expired era of sail. Rightfully these very rare but identifiable sailing workboats could be passed by as obsolete, but some old instruments of our past die very hard. The people who own and sail these remaining workboats live as marginally as do their boats. The ancient mariners of Sardinia cling to the older ways tenaciously. They have preserved for a few to see and still fewer to appreciate a very occasional ancient and deteriorated sailing coaster. They can be found here or there around the Ligurian Sea, in some out-of-the-way port of Corsica or even out in the Gulf of Lyon. These coasters are related to the Spanish feluccas used by Moorish pirates, which were related to the old galleys of Genoa, which in turn were related to the ships of the classical Mediterranean.

I remember quite vividly being moored many years ago in a small harbor on the Ligurian coast. It was a foul, cold night with a penetrating mist rain and a wind off the Maritime Alps that whipped across the harbor in sporadic blasts. It was sometime during the midwatch at an in-be-

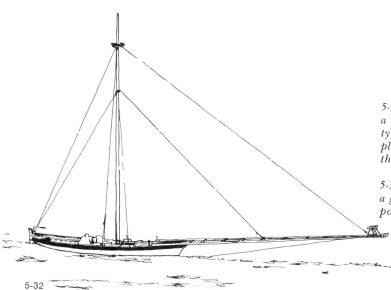

5-32

5-31　*An old-style Messina swordfishing boat — a low, graceful double ender. Boats of this type are generally rigged with a long bow platform and a harpoon pulpit. In the past, they approached their quarry under oars.*

5-32　*This type of large swordfishing boat with a greater pulpit extension and mechanical power is replacing the older harpoon boats.*

tween hour when all of the lights of yesterday had been extinguished ashore and none of the lights of tomorrow had yet been struck. The boatswain of my watch reported a dim light making into the harbor entrance. We identified it when it was finally within several hundred yards as a fishing vessel or coastwise boat of some local type. At about this point, the rattle of anchor chain was heard and the lone light was extinguished. The event was logged and forgotten momentarily. About a half hour later the boatswain reported that this craft was dragging anchor and was very close to colliding with us along our starboard side as we swung on our mooring. We attempted to hail her skipper but could not rouse him. I lit one of our large searchlights and told one of the men on watch to drop down from one of our boat booms on the deck of the old two master, where there now was a little dog running about creating his own confusion. At about this same time, the old boat's companion hatch squeaked open and a weathered face peered up with wide eyes staring in disbelief at the gray steel wall and forbidding naval guns beside and above him. The whole scene was illuminated by the blue glare of the searchlight beam on the black water around us. In another instant a young sailor joined his master on this slippery old wood deck below us and with an expressive stream of Italian oaths they got up their anchor, started a loud, one cylinder auxiliary, and disappeared quickly into the black wetness of the night.

It was not until this experience was over that I

5-33　*A Sardinian workboat. The boats of Sardinia are distinctly western Mediterranean in character. Unlike Sicilian boats, these are the same types of boats found along the Ligurian coast, the southern French coast, and the Spanish coast as far west as Malaga. Because the island of Sardinia is fairly isolated, the local boats are preserved and maintained well and still carry a single lateen sail for prime propulsion.*

5-33

143

5-34   A navicello sketched in 1937 when the type was fairly common. Now there are very few left.

5-35   The tartane originated from this small vessel of the Ligurian coast in the sixteenth century. It has a classic Mediterranean profile with its deep sheer, waist rail, and curving stem carrying a beak-like appendage.

5-36   The Italian tartana of the mid-seventeenth century traded throughout the Ligurian Sea and was the ancester of the nineteenth and twentieth century grande tartanes of the French and Italian coasts.

5-37   The grande tartane of southern France was a noble and proud boat. Its lofty lateen sail and large head sail (set flying) gave its sail plan a most pleasing and modern distribution. This is a profile of the boat at the beginning of the nineteenth century, but it remained the same for more than a century.

began to reflect that the boat of this encounter was unlike any boat in my limited knowledge. Having only been at that time in the Mediterranean a few months, I had not yet become very aware of the Mediterranean look in boats. I had never heard of a navicello of the Ligurian coast, and when, as on this craft, I observed the fore mast on a two-masted boat raking sharply forward, my first impression was that there had been an accident. With the coming of the clear, crisp morning this Italian navicello was revealed in all of her worn and mellowed glory, having anchored about a half mile away in the inner harbor beyond the mole. Later that day I went ashore and sketched as accurately as I could the impression of this boat which appears in Figure 5-34.

A navicello is most notable for its unusual rig. It formerly, perhaps only in the last century, was a lateener. The sails of the latter-day navicello are similar, in theory, to those of a staysail schooner, with two staysails between the masts set on upper and intermediate stays, a jib, set flying, and a large gaff mainsail. This boat also carries a large triangular topsail in light weather. It is comparatively large—65 to 70 feet long. The navicello was formerly used largely for transporting fine Italian marble from the ports near the Tuscan hills of Carrara. It must have been easy to carry her lofty rig with such ballast as Carrara marble. It is doubtful that many navicellos remain today.

Another coastwise boat of this region, which together with the navicello grew from a common ancestor, is the tartane (*tartana* in Italian). We

5-34

144

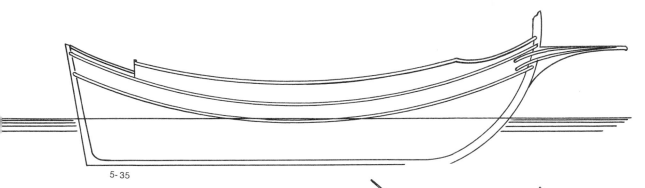

5-35

find in Chapman's *Architectura Navalis* a most graceful little Italian coaster of the 16th century identified as a tartana, with two masts carrying lateen sails and the foremast raked sharply forward. This foremast is not uncommon for the old lateeners, but it is a characteristic that was employed primarily by the larger fellucas and provincial barques. The profile of Chapman's tartana is very interesting in other respects, because the boat is so thoroughly Mediterranean in character and detail. In Figure 5-35, notice the raised washboard gunwale in the low sweep of her waist, the broad low rubwale, the rising stem post, and finally the projecting beak head. Only four centuries ago, this pretty little lateener, perhaps no more than 40 feet long, if that, was the prototype of all of the small coasters and traders of the western Mediterranean. The tartana was the forerunner of boats to come when the Mediterranean civilization shook off the bonds and restrictions of the medieval age and moved forward with the renaissance.

Small coasters such as the tartana could only grow larger and, in the process, experiment with mast and rig. One became the navicello; another became a more efficient single-masted lateener and was refined along the southern French coast to be the *grande tartane* of Provence. Figure 5-37 shows the profile of this handsome type at the apex of its development about 1800. The accompanying reproduction of Antoine Roux's watercolor of two tartanes, Figure 5-38, preserves his accurate impression of them under sail. A fishing tartane and

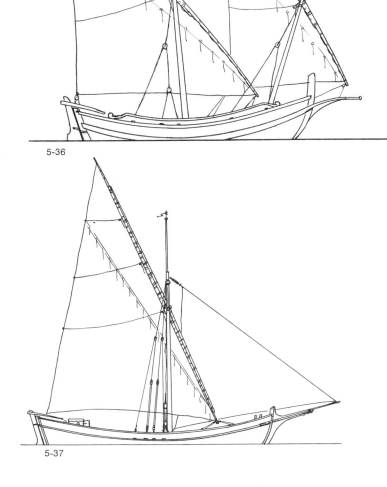

5-36

5-37

5-38

5-38 *Antoine Roux recorded two types of tartanes in 1816. The one on the left is a trader; the one on the right is a fisherman. The spinnaker set of the large headsails should be noted as well as the versatile use of water sails and topsails.*

5-39 *The twentieth century tartane developed into a poor, modified lateener that diminished in numbers after World War II. Today it is almost extinct. Note the use of the topsail with the lateen rig as if it were a gaff rig. This is unique with tartanes.*

a trading tartane demonstrate here the great versatility of their sails in good weather. Clearly shown here is a new refinement of the western Mediterranean lateen sail. From this painting it seems obvious that the sail and yard are held within tacking control on the *inside* of the running shrouds.

The tartane of the twenieth century was further refined and westernized to become a cutter-like lateener, with two headsails and a topsail set on the upper half of the lateen yard, as in the navicello. (See Figure 5-39.)

The tartane was of course a victim of her own affluence and impressive nineteenth century grandeur. In an age of commerce under sail, she had no peer in coastwise trade in the western Mediterranean. Sailing under French, Spanish, and Italian flags, and with slight ethnic differences, she was a dominant type for nearly two centuries. But now she is gone except perhaps for an occasional isolated remnant or mastless hull. I saw two under sail in 1939 near Genoa and made the hasty sketch shown here. Two or three apparently survived after World War II.

Besides the tartane, there is a smaller, poorer type of lateener in the Ligurian region. Normally just called a Tuscan coaster, she carries a single, heavy, forward-raked mast in the ancient manner with a heavy lateen yard. There is usually a long bowsprit which pushes forward a large triangular headsail set flying from a toggle on a masthead halyard. The Tuscan coaster has a shapely, beamy hull with deep gunwales and a raised,

capped stem post. The outboard rudder is swung on a nearly vertical stern post with a tiller crossing above. She makes a very pleasing picture with her nicely proportioned rig and stained sail pushing down the coast with a northwesterly kicking up a sea behind her and the mountainous coast ahead. Such boats are 45 to 50 feet in length and are built according to the rules of tradition and their builder's critical eye. A very similar boat found in the Gulf of Lyon is a fishing lateener called a bateau boeuf. Originally this boat was a poor man's tartane and was used in the coastwise trade. It is today almost obsolete.

Farther to the west, beyond the Gulf of Lyon, large lateen fishing boats indigenous to the coast of Catalonia are still in use. This coast has few natural harbors, aside from the great port of Barcelona, and, for the most part, is a rocky coastline that is punctured by small sandy coves which lend themselves well to beaching boats. There are great stretches of beach strands as well, and for centuries the Catalonian fishermen have been hauling their boats up these sunny, sandy shelves. The boats here are of several sizes, the largest being 35 to 40 feet in length. The style is one of ruggedness, generally with a forward-raking mast and a single lateen sail. The boats today are also motorized and all have a large, protected propeller aperature. Figure 5-42 shows one of these hulls stripped down for painting, with a nice but patched job of carvel planking exposed. The

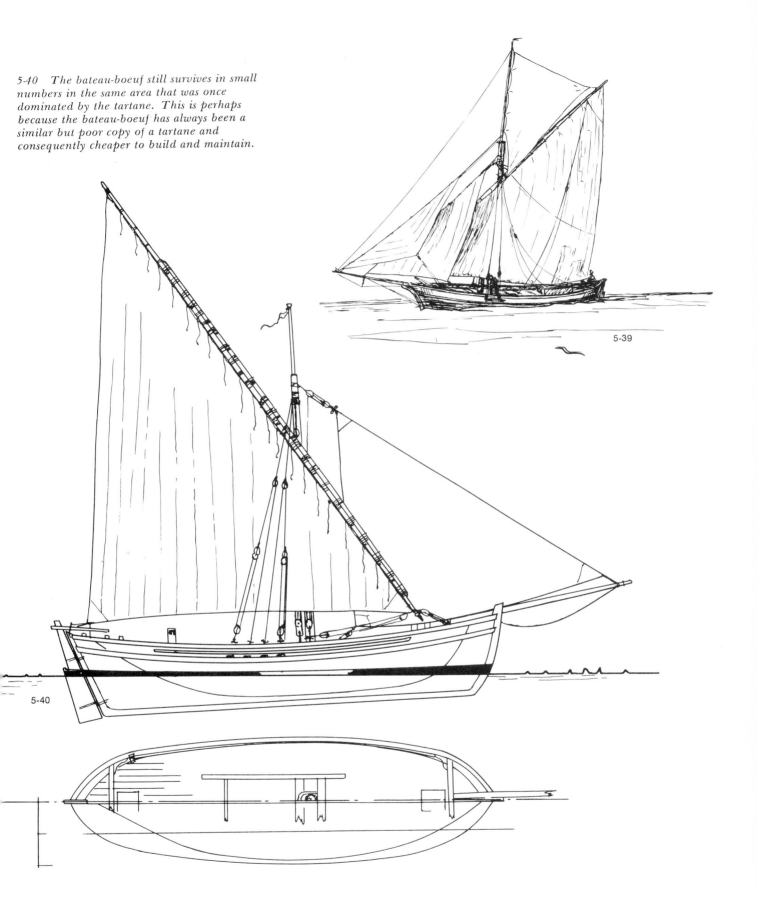

5-40 *The bateau-boeuf still survives in small numbers in the same area that was once dominated by the tartane. This is perhaps because the bateau-boeuf has always been a similar but poor copy of a tartane and consequently cheaper to build and maintain.*

5-39

5-40

5-41 Balearic Island fishing craft are typical western Mediterranean boats with a few local variations. Their stems are vertical and without curvature. Their keels have little rocker and there is a bit more flare in their bow sections. The acetylene stern lantern for night fishing is standard equipment on coastal boats from Italy, France and Spain.

5-42 The hull of a Catalonian beach-operated lateener, a boat that follows strictly the tradition of the western Mediterranean. This is a rugged but shapely double ender, heavily built with a flush deck below her deep gunwales. Note the heavy beaching keels. The sailing rig is a single lateen without headsail on a mast raked forward in the centuries-old style. Most of this type of boat depend nowadays on a heavy semi-diesel or gasoline engine only.

5-43 This beach boat of southern France has a "chicken beak," a form found throughout the ages on Mediterranean craft.

5-44 The harbor and beach boat of Genoa is typified by the inward curves of her extended stem and stern posts.

5-42

smaller Catalonian boats are about 15 to 17 feet long and are generally rowed. All are open with only partial decks and deep gunwales. They always have heavy, bilge keels for beaching, which, together with the structural keel, are on the same horizontal plane.

The boats of Valencia and the Balearic Islands to the south of Catalonia are of similar style, but of an intermediate size, between 25 and 30 feet. Figure 5-41 shows a typical motorized fishing boat of Mallorca entering Puerto Soller.

The boats that have occupied our attention for the past several pages are of a most typical western Mediterranean model. With only slight regional variations, most of the boats of all types from Tunis to Gibraltar are of this same form and style. Besides the characteristic double-ended form, the most common element of this Middle Sea style is the raised stem post with a decorative cap. In some regions, such as in the vicinity of Genoa, the stem post as well as the stern post are raked sharply inward. (See Figure 5-44.) Occasionally on some small beach craft or harbor craft one may encounter a very curious and useless remnant of ancient Mediterranean ship construction—the forward thrusting beakhead (see Figure 5-43). This remnant is not confined to the western Mediterranean alone and was mentioned in connection with the Turkish taka. The beakhead is apparently a hangover from the days when it was the forward-jutting stem platform of Venetian

5-41

5-43

galleys or fifteen century naos (medieval Mediterranean trading ships). It was used on the early renaissance tartana, and in the last tartanes became a type of clipper bow. It is not, however, a clipper bow; at least not of a Yankee clipper. There is strong evidence to warrant belief that this forward-raking stem on the old galleys of Venice was adopted from the classic triremes of Rome and ancient Greece where this structure was truly a beak. As a ram, it was an effective weapon. It originated in the early centuries of the second millennium B.C.

The ubiquitous, graceful little beach boats are the smallest and most purely Mediterranean of all of the indigenous boats in this great blue sea. They come in many sizes and colors. Some are bright and new, others are old and shabby, and all suggest styles of centuries past.

There are few if any boats on the North African side of the Mediterranean that have any indigenous quality not already noted as a general Mediterranean quality. The boats of Morocco are mostly Spanish-Mediterranean. The boats of Algeria are very like the French beach boats of the Riviera, to be described below, except they are not maintained as well. The boats of Tunisia are largely Italian in form and structure. There is, however, in Tunis an interesting small beach boat of Italian origin that is no longer to be found in Italy. It is called a *martiqana* and originated in the lower Adriatic region as far up as Brindisi. The boats were not too long ago quite capable sailboats of the indigenous Adriatic lugger type.

5-44

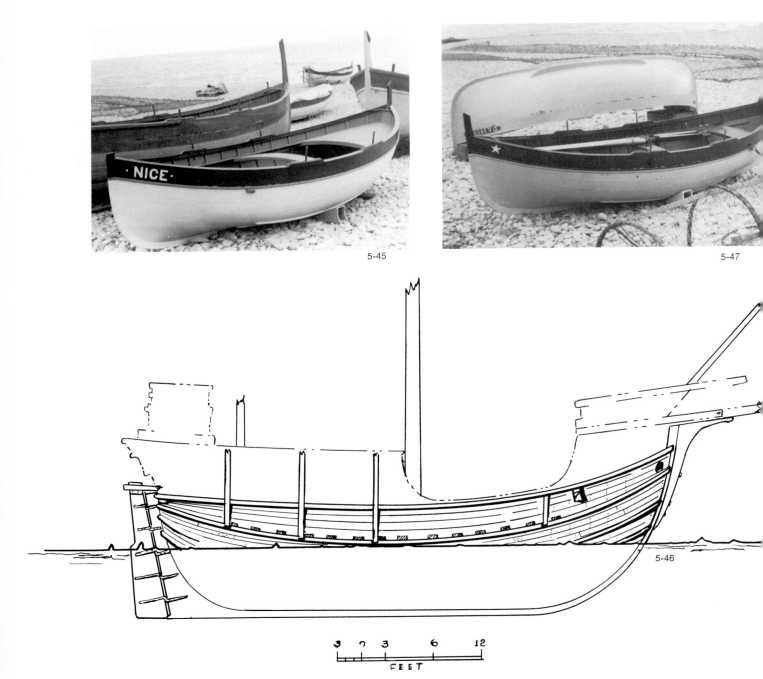

5-45

5-47

5-46

3 2 3 6 12
FEET

5-45 Beach boats of the French Mediterranean coast.

5-46 While the false stem knee may have some remote connection to an ancient ram, it is more likely a holdover from medieval ships. This profile of a fifteenth century nao shows the clear and functional use of the stem knee that later evolved into a type of "clipper" bow (as it became known in America).

5-48

5-47 *The smallest French beach boats are very much like Maine peapods, with a few distinctive Mediterranean touches. These boats are seldom more than 12 feet long. They are in their own way the classic essence of carvel boat form as is the Norway skiff of the north.*

5-48 *The small harbor boats seen on the Costa Brava of Spain and to the south and west of Barcelona are slightly different in form and more rugged than the French version.*

The boats generally are under 30 feet in length, but some have been built up to 40 feet. They have the typical deep, narrow rudder of the trabaccolo and are of similar shallow construction. The comparative lightness of the boats is essential because of the beach operations. The most identifiable feature is the distinctive raked-out "clipper"-type stem knee. This feature, which is noted elsewhere in this chapter on Turkish, Greek, and French boats, is unique on a boat originating in the Adriatic.

Among the great works of art, there are many contemporary representations of small workboats. Very few are painted with technical accuracy. Because many of these artists were of Mediterranean heritage, there are many scenes that include local Mediterranean watercraft. However, it is unusual to find an indigenous Mediterranean boat painted by an artist who is not from the Mediterranean, who is an impressionist, and whose drawing in this context is fairly accurate in detail and form. The color, composition, and grace of the boats in Vincent van Gogh's well known "Beach of Saintes Maries" contribute altogether to the total aesthetic quality of the painting. The execution of the boats in this painting, when they are examined closely, reveals the artist's competent eye for accuracy and detail. He certainly did not make these boats out of his imagination. He painted them quite truly from life. The unstudied but natural placement of an oar or casually dropped coil of line, the inside of the transom, the curve of plank and frame, are all very real in this painting.

Yet the bright colors and slightly exaggerated forms of the boats create an other-world unreality, causing some knowledgeable people to dismiss the boats as figments of Van Gogh's mind.

It is quite true that boats like these rendered by Van Gogh in the 1870's no longer exist in Saintes Maries, France, or anywhere for that matter. They did, however, exist there at one time along these beaches near the Rhone estuary west of Marseille. The beaches are wide and flat in this delta land, and the boats undoubtedly had to be flat and keelless like a dory. They were definitely large, colorfully painted sailing "dories" with single lateen sails on long willowy yards. Today, there is nothing left of such boats, except for a very few power fishing and harbor craft of a very similar model in and around Marseille. They are identified by American sailors as Marseille dories. One of these boats can be seen among others tied up in the inner harbor quay of Marseille (See Figure 5-49). Marseille dories are about 18 feet in length and 6 feet in beam. They have the natural sweep of sheer created by the flat, flaring sides of this elemental boat form. The ends are double and the bottom is flat, with the gentle fore-and-aft rocker of all dories. The freeboard is increased by a raised gunwale plank with tumblehome, which is tapered off at the ends. Except for its dory-form, the Marseille dory is thoroughly Mediterranean in construction. Without doubt it is the rare existing relative of the brightly colored boats painted by Van Gogh on the beach of Les Saintes Maries one hundred years ago.

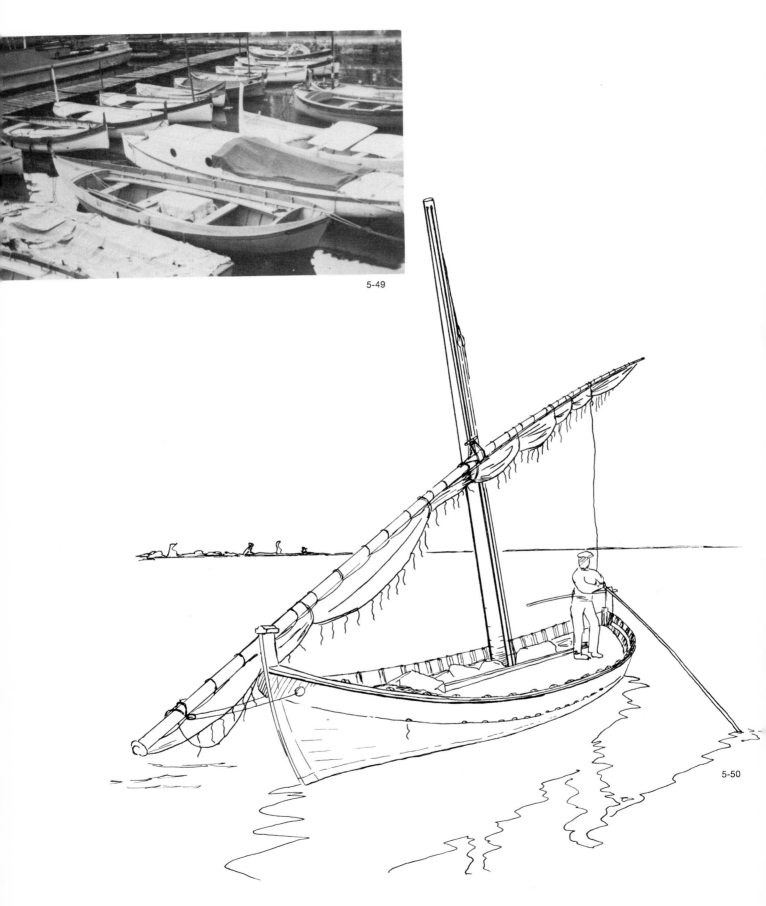

5-49

5-50

5-49   The Marseille dory with its straight
sections stands out from the other
Mediterranean craft in this photograph. These
dories, with their original lateen rigs, are the
boats of Van Gogh's famous painting of the
beach of Saintes Maries.

5-50   The Valencia lake barge, which is less a
barge than it is a graceful double ender, is a
classic lateener carrying a typical forward-raking
mast and single sail. Its work is mainly
transporting oranges across Lake Albufera.

5-51   The Tunisian lateen-rigged coaster has
a square-transom stern, a ketch-type sail
arrangement, and a large headsail.

It must be apparent at this point that in the Mediterranean there are different forces at work that shape the boats and preserve them. There is very little economic incentive to support or encourage new construction. Where truly indigenous qualities were observed (aside from Turkey), they appeared most predominantly in the smallest craft. In the Mediterranean, existing watercraft are simply a manifestation of historic truths. The political and cultural conditions of communities are reflected in the arts and crafts of their working people and are generally an indication of their national progress.

The Mediterranean Sea is bordered by many countries of various and conflicting political persuasions. The former coastwise trade has in this century been supplanted by international and intercontinental trade carried by many other more efficient transporters. With modern trucks, cargo planes, railways, and large freighters in use, there is little need for small coastwise cargo vessels. The fisheries of the Mediterranean are limited, indeed, and can only support local markets and limited numbers of independent fishermen—hence the concentration on small fishing boats and beach craft. There is no demand for great numbers of herring trawlers or drifters on this sea like those supporting large industries in many northern countries.

This is the picture of today's workboats in a sea where once there was a proliferation of indigenous small craft engaged in so many types of water commerce. The Mediterranean has not lost its his-

toric significance as a stage for the flexing of international sea power. It has simply moved to a dependency on participants who are not of the Mediterranean world and on vessels far too large and complex to have been developed in any one locality.

5-51

IT IS NOT KNOWN definitely which civilization was the first to settle on the shores of the Iberian Peninsula. The Phoenicians and later the Carthaginians, however, established outposts on the Spanish Mediterranean coast as well as the Atlantic coast of Portugal. It is a reasonable conclusion from this that the early boatbuilding practices of this entire region were derived from the Mediterranean.

Let us imagine a scene 3,000 years ago of a Phoenician trading boat drawn up high on a sunny, sandy shore of the Spanish coast. The very few crew members are, in their self-sufficient fashion, restoring a sick bottom plank and tightening the caulking between others, having scraped clean the entire barnacled surface. The boat itself is nicely constructed with sawn frames and smooth but worn carvel planks. She has high ends with a dominant stem post rising at the bow and graceful inward-curving stern post. Her forefoot and keel are of heavy timber, nicely scarfed to shape a fine entrance. Her deck is set from stem to stern on heavy beams which notch through the side planks. (This practice began with the ancient Egyptians and persisted in both southern and northern European boats for nearly 30 centuries.) The old boat's deck is well below the sheer line, making a deep, protective gunwale. She carries double king posts at the bow on both sides of the stem. Her single mast, normally stepped amidships, has been lowered and is temporarily serving as a ridge pole for a striped awning. This fabric that provides protection against the burning Mediterranean sun is normally the single sail and is nicely sewn and roped. It is adequate in area to cover most of the boat's deck. Her cargo has been unloaded on the beach. With an assortment of rope, line, and other gear strewn at random on the sand, the men work leisurely at the task of getting out and fitting a new plank while the master checks his valuable items of trade for restowage. The shipwright's tools that are skillfully turned to the repair work are the basic adze, the caulking iron (actually bronze) and mallet, bow-saw, draw knife, chisels, and block plane. The entire scene, with the exception of the language and the dress of the people, is timeless on these Iberian shores.

The detailed shape of the boat and her protruding deck beam structure has, during the millenniums, been refined. The boat's cargo and freight equipment have been replaced with traditional fishing gear, but the boats of today on all coasts of the Iberian Peninsula have the same basic characteristics of the 3,000-year-old boat just described. The high stem posts still dominate the sweeping sheer line; the stern posts still curve inward; the sides and bottoms are smoothly planked and caulked; and the frames are sawn and closely spaced. The boats are still built in the open, most frequently on a sandy beach front using the same basic tools. The rugged keel and scarfed stem and stern post are shaped into an easy, fine entrance. This bow form, so fundamental, yet with so many variations, originated on the eastern shore of the Mediterranean.

The boats built today along the southern shores

6-1   The hull form of this Spanish trawler
makes her suitable for extended operations.
Her design is undoubtedly influenced by other
seagoing trawlers as well as the universal
requirements of trawling itself. The heavy
trawler stern and forward-raking stem post are
characteristics of Spanish and Portuguese
construction and are found in some of the
largest vessels still being built of wood.

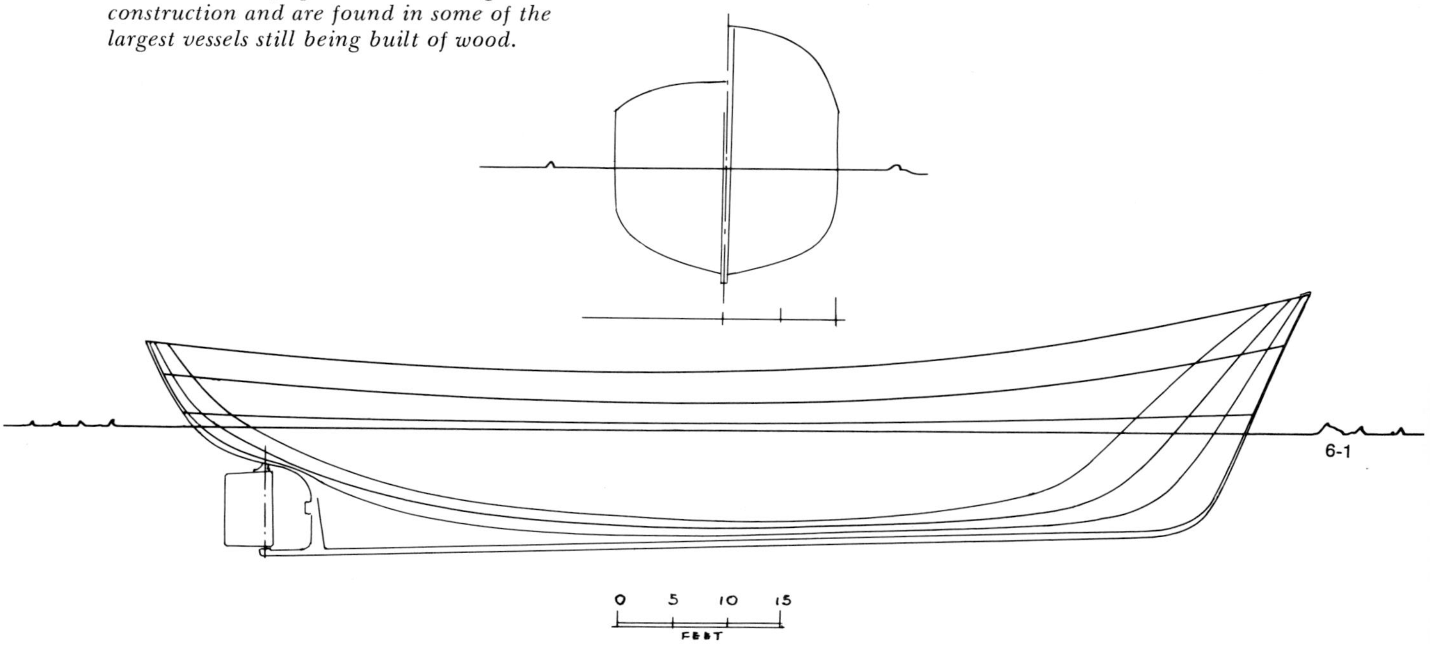

6-1

0   5   10   15
FEET

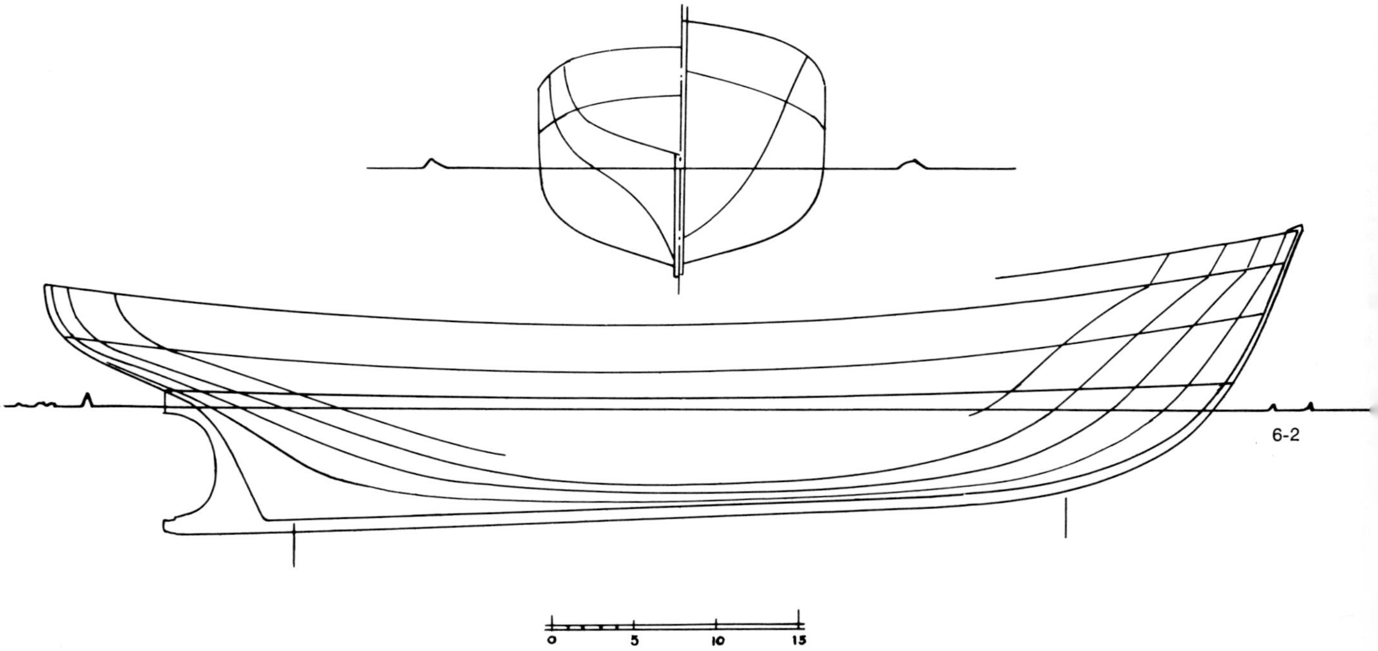

6-2

0   5   10   15

6-3

6-2 Italian seiners and trawlers are similar in style to the Spanish boats but generally show more grace and lift of line. This seiner has the customary Italian counter stern instead of a trawler stern.

6-3 Small Spanish tuna boats. These are really combination boats, because when tuna are scarce they turn to sardines, squid, and bottomfish.

of Spain are larger than the boats of the Catalonian coast discussed previously, and are used for the sardine fisheries. These boats are built mainly to the south of the Gulf of Valencia in the region of Alicante. They are fairly large craft designed for seining with heavy, large nets. The shape of these boats is a departure from the classic Mediterranean style just described only in that the modern boats have a broad, overhanging counter stern to provide a good working platform. The stem rakes sharply forward and the bows show a great flare in the forward sections. The boats measure generally 60 to 65 feet in length with a beam of approximately 20 feet. This type of boat will be further described on subsequent pages on the boats of Portugal, where sardine seiners of the same identity are built. The boat as built and working in Spain is the most substantial of all contemporary working boats built in the western Mediterranean, and its likeness to the Portuguese sardine boats points up the common motivations, historical forces, and traditions that appear in all the Iberian boats. Typical hull lines are shown in Figure 6-1. The same build is evident in the boats in the Bay of Biscay. The most characteristic feature is the flaring bow section above the deck level (see Figure 6-3).

Fine sardine seiners are built, and have been built in the past, in Spain and Italy. However, because these countries are diversified industrial countries with comparatively minor fishing industries, more interesting boats are found along the Portuguese coast.

Since the first sea trade routes were extended from the Mediterranean to northern Europe, without interruption for some 3,000 or more years, the Atlantic coast of Portugal has offered its natural harbors, its protected beaches, and its great river estuaries to countless laden boats and ships. The Romans called this land Lusitania and established it as part of their colonial empire. It was colonized before the Romans by Greeks and Carthaginians, who found Phoenician outposts already there. The Phoenicians undoubtedly followed the Minoans, first through the straits in search of tin and copper. But not until comparatively recent centuries did Portugal become the crossroads between northern and southern Europe, or a point of departure for exploration to the south and the west. At the mouth of the great Tagus River, where there is a broad, protected estuary, the Romans built their town, which is now called Lisbon. The river flows down from far across central Spain, bisecting Portugal, and at last falling into the great harbor basin of Lisbon, where the current just before the river joins the ocean is nearly nine knots.

It is here in this magnificent natural harbor, which attracts ships of all flags, that there has long been a use for harbor lighters and small cargo-transfer craft. The Tagus River sailing barges, relative to the harbor craft and barges of other great world seaports, are the most colorful, carefully constructed, and well maintained of them all. The sampans of Shanghai, the caiques of Istanbul, the gaiassas of Cairo, and the Thames sailing barges

6-4 *A ribetejo boat, a Tagus River lighter, whose extreme raking mast, shorter gaff, and carved and curving stem post set it apart from the frigata.*

6-5 *The sailing lighters of Lisbon are a familiar sight but few visitors look closely at them. The tradition of their colorful decoration goes back thousands of years. This boat is a frigata, distinguished by its severe lines, plumb stem, and broad transom stern.*

of London cannot stand up to the still-active Tagus River craft in character and capability.

There are two quite distinct types of sailing lighters on the Tagus estuary. The names are not descriptive, only generic, but they are more useful identifying labels than the words barge or lighter. These boats are not lighters or barges in the conventionally accepted meaning, which usually indicates large flat-bottom scow-like vessels for carrying bulk cargo, often with no means of self-propulsion. On the contrary, while these harbor boats of the Tagus carry all types of cargo, they have shapely and finely constructed hulls propelled by handsome spreads of sail from single masts.

The type called a frigata is the heavier and fuller of the two; it is some 45 feet in length and 15 feet in beam. (See Figure 6-5.) Her hull is heavily constructed against the hard usage she suffers amidst the crowding of the harbor. She has heavy double kingposts on her bow rails and similar square bollards on the stern rails; she also has a very steep but natural sheer line which drops from her stem, tends to flatten amidships and rise only slightly at the stern. Her hold area extends throughout the waist and is entirely open with only flat removable flooring in the bottom. The stem rises vertically and straight and projects in the Mediterranean manner, while the stern has a broad transom with an outboard rudder. The rudder has a high, painted head, and the tiller passes inboard above a broad quarterdeck. Below this deck is a small unlighted cabin area. The raking

mast just forward of amidships hoists a well-cut gaff mainsail with a fairly long gaff and loose foot. While the sail is hooped to the mast, it is seldom lowered but rather brailed in. There is a single staysail and no bowsprit. This boat makes leeway in a manner that would not delight a yachtsman, but when beating across the Tagus' current on a brisk onshore breeze this can be forgiven. The boat is characteristically decorated in many colors, often in shades of blue with details painted in yellow, red, and black and bordered in white. The rudderhead and interior main deck beam facings are always carved and painted in intricate floral designs. The frigata's most impressive feature is her broad, powerful bow, which most certainly was developed to counter the steep chop in the Tagus' mouth when the wind and current cross.

The ribetejo boat, the other harbor type, is about the same length as the frigata but is generally not as broad or heavy, although heavy enough for its lusty employment. The general appearance of this boat is more suggestive of Portuguese antiquity than is that of the frigata (see Figure 6-4). The single-masted rig is very similar to the frigata's, except that it sometimes carries two headsails, both from inboard headstays with no bowsprit. The mainsail, also set on an aft-raking mast, often has a shorter gaff reminiscent of the Dutch bezan rig. Both of these Lisbon harbor boats were originally lateen rigged, but in this century, the Lisbon sailors have apparently become convinced that, for working in crowded harbor conditions

6-4

6-5

159

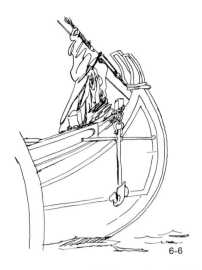

6-6

6-6 The double-carved stem of a ribetejo boat. It is as though the heavy sheer rail is trying to combine with the extended stem post. This same style is repeated in several other old Portuguese boats.

6-7 The Peniche sardine carrier is identified by its unusually long counter stern. This broad overhang makes a convenient net-handling platform for the fishermen to work from at sea. It also contributes to dryness when the boat is stern launched from the beach.

6-8 A seiner under construction. Note the heavy, closely spaced sawn frames. This type of boat must be rugged to cope with beach operations.

with much tacking, the all-inboard gaff rig is more accommodating and workable.

The bow construction of the ribetejo boat is most curious (see Figure 6-6). The stem profile is rounded in a near semicircle from the keel to the upper terminus. The sheer line rises sharply in an upcurve, with its heavy gunwale timber continuing over the stempost and up its forward face. The profile of this whole upper structure curves back on an inward slope. The resulting assembly is one that has not been seen on a boat since the Greek boats of the third century B.C. sailed from the Aegean. The most puzzling thing about this similar profile on Greek boats is that it was a feature of their sterns, not their bows. It is consequently difficult to speculate about the origin of the Portuguese ribetejo bow. We know that Greeks and Carthaginians voyaged, traded, and settled on the Tagus before the Romans. The appearance of the rising ends of their boats may have made a very strong and lasting impression on the Portuguese. If this stem were used only on the ribetejo boat in Portugal, it could be passed off as a local aberration. This is not the case, however, for there are other boats in the northern part of Portugal on the Atlantic coast with the same type of stem decoration. These boats work from the beaches and lagoons of Aveiro and will be described in fuller detail later.

To the north of Lisbon the shores are inhospitable with high rocky cliffs and open beaches. The Atlantic Ocean waves have a fetch of 3,000 miles before they beat upon this coast. Yet there are many fishing villages, and the fishing industry contributes greatly to the Portuguese economy. Needless to say, the fishermen are a tough breed, their boats are strong and well adapted, and their wives frequently wear black. Many vacationers can be found in the summertime in these fishing ports along the fine sandy beaches below the dark cliffs. This is not surprising because the surf is generally up, the sand is white and fine, and the sun shines warmly. But still the sea is the Atlantic and not the Mediterranean; the Portuguese fishing villages of Nazaré, Peniche, and Ericeira are not Riviera towns like Saint-Tropez, Antibes, or Portofino. The best boats grow on the most rugged sea coast and, unlike garden vegetables, are nurtured in the most unkindly weather. In the worst months of the winter in Portugal, during the great Atlantic storms, the boats are drawn up high on the beaches, or where the beaches are inadequate, they are sweated up steep ramps to cliff tops or even as in Nazaré, drawn up on the streets of the town.

One cannot look at any Portuguese working boats and not be strongly impressed with their ruggedness and fine maintenance. Especially impressive is the efficient performance of the fishermen with their boats.

On the beaches of the fishing village of Peniche sardine seiners can be found that are very similar in style and appearance to the Spanish seiners described previously in this chapter. They are slightly smaller than the Spanish seiners and some

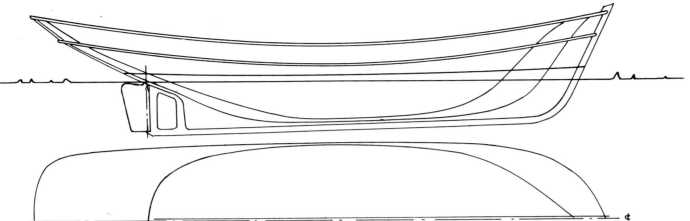

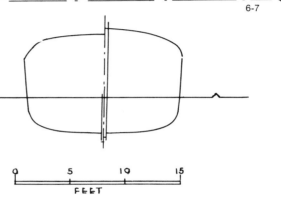

6-7

times feature a broader elliptical stern. Figure 6-7 illustrates the lines and form of these seiners. These boats, like their Spanish relatives, and, for that matter, all of the working boats of Portugal, are built in the open, often on the beach, sometimes with a temporary canvas shelter providing shade from the sun. The builders work, as is common in southern Europe, from experience and by eye, using knowledge that is centuries old and is passed on to them orally. Their creativity and imagination, however, are not totally overshadowed by traditional methods. The sardine seiners of Peniche and Sesimbra are boats of relatively modern configuration and have evolved as power-driven boats with very little suggestion of their sailing ancestors.

Figure 6-8 shows one of these seiners being constructed near Setubal, south of Lisbon. The heavy, closely spaced frames can be seen above the deck level, where they are not doubled as they are in the body of the hull below. The forward-raking stem is characteristic of these boats as is the broad, overhanging elliptical stern. The boat under construction here is typical and measures about 55 feet overall length, 15 feet beam, and 4.5 feet mean draft. It is typical not only of this region of Portugal but of the sardine seiners of the whole southern coast of Iberia. These boats in Portugal alone are responsible for landing about 150,000 tons of sardines annually, worth as much as 20 million dollars to the nation's economy.

While these sardine seiners are typical of Iberia and are hard-working, excellent sea boats, they are

6-8

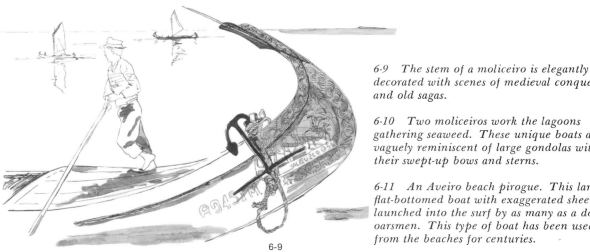

6-9

6-9 *The stem of a moliceiro is elegantly decorated with scenes of medieval conquests and old sagas.*

6-10 *Two moliceiros work the lagoons gathering seaweed. These unique boats are vaguely reminiscent of large gondolas with their swept-up bows and sterns.*

6-11 *An Aveiro beach pirogue. This large flat-bottomed boat with exaggerated sheer is launched into the surf by as many as a dozen oarsmen. This type of boat has been used from the beaches for centuries.*

contemporary boats that do not have the traditional heritage and character of most of the rest of the small Portuguese workboats.

On the Atlantic coast near the town of Aveiro, the sandy beaches flatten out to form broad, protected lagoons. Because of the proximity of the sea, there are large accumulations of seaweed in these lagoons which is of considerable value in agriculture. The collection and transportation of the seaweed is accomplished by boats, and these boats are perhaps the most unusually formed and decorated class of sailing workboats in use in the western world. They are called moliceiros because of their employment in transporting molicos (seaweed). Their movement about the lagoons and canals reminds one of Holland and Venice. Aveiro itself resembles a Dutch city with canals, houses, and waterfront stores of Dutch facade.

The moliceiros are basically shallow-draft, lug-rigged lighters from 35 to 55 feet in length. They are open in the waist and when loaded seem nearly awash. Their most astonishing and perhaps most handsome feature is their upswept ends and "back-swept," decorated stem. From a distance there is no doubt that a moliceiro is a very graceful and well-proportioned craft (see Figure 6-10). Most of them are single masted, but the larger ones are two-masted, with the fore being the smaller. The rig is somewhat like the bragozzo of Venice, with the smaller of the two lugsails being forward and without any staysail or headsails of any kind. It is a basic lug-rig form, similar to the rig of eastern Mediterranean craft three millenniums ago.

The stem form of the moliceiro sketched in Figure 6-9, is reminiscent of the after end of a gondola, but it is my conviction that it's origin is far, far older. The combination of stem and sheer plank extension that was noted in the ribetejo boats of Lisbon is apparent. On the sides of each bow extending four or five feet abaft the stem head, there is an area of detailed pictorial decoration. The style of figures, both human and animal, is medieval in technique and application. The abstract figures of the border of these decorations seem to be older and, while documentation is not possible, there is an obvious similarity to eastern Mediterranean decorations originating on the Phoenician and Syrian coasts at the end of the second pre-Christian millennium.

It is most curious that the cut and set of the lugsails on the moliceiros are a combination of the northern and southern lug. The sail is boomless at the foot and tacked down at the mast. The sail is not dipped around the mast in tacking. The large, high rudder is most impressive, but the skippers are most casual about using it, staying at the helm only when maneuvering in canals. The moliceiro is an old, useful, and handsome boat and still most functional. Its light and simple flat-bottom structure, however, eliminates it from any work beyond canals and lagoons.

Near this same region, at Costa Nova, there is a sea boat which has much of the form and decorations of the moliceiro. The nearest thing that I could learn for a name to call them sounded much like "pirogue." They are perhaps similar to a

6-10

6-11

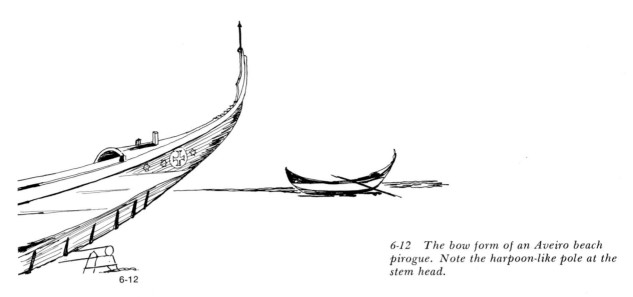

6-12 *The bow form of an Aveiro beach pirogue. Note the harpoon-like pole at the stem head.*

French sailor's fancy of a great canoe. These boats are of stronger construction than the lagoon boats, but they are also flat-bottomed with high ends, actually a much higher bow than the moliceiro. These beach-operated fishing craft are launched through surf, as is the general custom along the Portuguese coast, and the excessive sheer is no doubt the result of this requirement. Even so, the sheer is definitely exaggerated when compared to other boats of similar requirements. It is my conviction that, because the boats are economically built and flat on the bottom for standing up on the hard sand, their quarter-moon sheer profile fulfills the demand for a form of natural strength. The characteristic shape can be seen in Figure 6-11.

Figure 6-12 is fairly representative of these surf pirogues. While the sheer curvature is unusual, the general profile of these boats shows they are well suited for their use. They are approximately 50 feet in length overall but no more than 27 on the waterline. They are, and surely must always have been, powered by oars. The bow is far higher than the stern, which is an obvious indication of their daily engagement with the nearly ever-present surf. But beyond the mere loftiness of the stem, the pirogue also has, like the moliceiro of the lagoons and the ribetejo boat of the Tagus, the curious extension of stem and sheerwale. And also, as though more is needed at this extremity, the stem head, which is perhaps 12 feet above the water, is surmounted by a harpoon-like pole. This latter appendage is for the showing of a signal, the purpose of which, I, at least, will have to admit,

is known only to the sailors of Costa Nova. One might wonder from the description and sketch of this high-ended boat how a man could manage to get out on this stem if he must set this "signal," work a net, or scan the sea for fish. There is indeed a series of steps fashioned into the upper and outermost end of the stem where the forward deck blends into it.

The decorations of the surf-pirogue seem less lavish and a bit cruder than those of the lagoon boats; the old Maltese and medieval cross form with six-pointed and five-pointed stars are used.

There is nothing lost in colorful, compassionate, and reassuring names used for these boats. Generally throughout all fishing communities, the boats' names are quite naturally genuine statements of some affection either to person or diety. The Portuguese sailors are often more involved than most in such traditions—perhaps rightly so because of their complete and constant devotion to church and the elemental sea. However, two examples of typical boat names on the Costa Nova strand, rather directly translated, are: *Day-after-day-life-goes-off* and *God-help-him-who-has-to-work*. Such names contrast with a less reverent *Linda Darnell*, seen on a small beach boat some 100 miles along the shore to the south.

Both the lagoon boats of Aveiro and the nearby high-ended surf boats are from the same heritage, preserved through the years by the same traditions, economic fortunes and failures, and historic events that came and went. They are living, moving, solid monuments to an age that never was as they combine so many mixed ages in their unique forms and decorations. They are only suggestions of both the recent past and dim antiquity. We can say now that they have been successful, because they are still graceful and functional forms.

Down the coast from the beaches of Aveiro, there is an impressive, rocky promontory rising four hundred feet above the sandy beach and jutting out into the sea like a great, ancient, crumbling jetty of a race of giants. Immediately under the protection of this promontory on the south spreads one of the loveliest beaches of all Portugal and the fishing community of Nazaré. But because the wind is generally from the west, this natural barrier to the northerlies does not prevent surf.

Along these beaches there is a special breed of fisherman and likewise special breeds of boats. The assortment of boat types in use at Nazaré is surprising; there are normally to be seen, either on the beach, coming or going, or lying offshore, five identifiable styles of indigenous boats. Because launching operations are entirely off the open beach, the largest craft is not more than 50 feet in length, and boats this size are not frequently launched. Altogether, there are about 200 boats operating from this beach during the season.

The sardine seiners are the largest boats and are the same as those described earlier as coming from Peniche, which lies only about twenty-five miles down the coast to the south.

The next largest boat is open and pulled by eight to ten oars. It is high-ended, has a round bilge, and has a forward-raking stem. The boats of this type vary in size from 30 to 35 feet, and are used for managing long drift nets in conjunction with other boats. At first glance it seems to be only a heavily constructed large surf boat of graceful line that features a swept-up sheer line forward and a projecting stem post. There is present in some of these boats a curious and provocative construction detail that is apparent to those who look a second time and have an eye for ancient details. Some of these boats stand alone with a basic part of their structure apparently the same as that of the most ancient of all wood-planked boats.

In the ancient Egyptian temple of Deir el Bahari in the Nile valley there is a row of stone reliefs dating from 1500 B.C. showing clearly the boats of Queen Hatshepsut with the great detail that the Egyptian artists liked to show in profile. Among other details in the construction of these boats, there is the depiction of projecting beam heads along the sheer at about the level of the deck. These are obviously the ends of deck beams projecting through the side planking, where, being securely pinned, they held together the boat's skin and kept it from spreading and sagging. These beam ends are also apparent in frescoes and reliefs showing Phoenician ships of the same period. They are very evident in the war boats of Pharaoh Ramses III as pictured in his tomb of 1200 B.C This type of construction, however, was not to be abandoned easily, because it is later apparent in the paintings of the galleys of classic

6-13   The beach boats of Nazaré are smaller
than those of Aveiro but are more varied. This
heavy double-ended boat is much like a large
whale boat with a deep body. The thwarts
and transverse deck members are brought
through the planking and pinned on the
outside.

6-14   A Nazaré beach boat.

6-13

166

6-14

Greece and still later in the bronze reliefs showing Roman war galleys as well as merchant vessels from the pre-Christian era through the third century A.D.

This structural feature must have been a very fundamental doctrine of shipbuilding—not just of the ancient Mediterranean world — because it spread to the medieval ships of northern Europe which were planked Nordic fashion, with lapped strakes. This construction is evident in the thirteenth century English ships and the Hanseatic cogs, as shown on the official seals of the Cinque Ports and Hanseatic League cities. Most ships' structures continued to be held by these externally-pinned-through beams until the sixteenth century, when the great carracks and caravels used the added outside wales and massive hanging knees which tied the deck beams to the frames internally. Since that time ships and boats built of wood have, in the western and eastern worlds (as far as we can tell), adopted this far more logical, completely internal frame structure with only minor local variations—but not some of the large, surf-launched fishing boats of Nazaré. The *Maria Eulalia* in Figure 6-13 was observed in the spring of 1970. The projecting beam ends with through pins are unmistakable along the white gunwale.

The boat in Figure 6-14 is of the same type but the beam ends discussed above are not visible because they are covered by discarded auto tires as fenders along her side. The open, oar-propelled, surf-launched fishing boat of Nazaré is unique to these central fishing beaches of Portugal. It is not found elsewhere, and only rarely beyond twenty kilometers north or south of Nazaré. On the beach here below the rocky promontory there can be counted perhaps ten to fifteen of this design. Like all Portuguese boats their hulls are brightly painted in reds, blues, yellows, and other colors, often with a contrasting sheer stripe. There is often a wedge-shaped area of color at both forward and after ends running up from the waterline and sloping away to the under side of the rubwale. This same form of decoration and style of painting is used in the boats of Malta. There are other decorations both in boats and ashore, such as the similarity of the crosses, that reflect the historic relationship between Portugal and Malta. The beach boats of Portugal, such as those in Nazaré, have no Maltese counterpart, however, for there is no Atlantic surf in Malta nor great open beaches of sand to draw up on. One of these boats, with seven or eight men at the oars and an additional nine or ten fishermen embarked, pointing its rising bow at a cresting breaker, is an image of everlasting seamanship.

There are two other types of smaller boats operated off Nazaré's beach; one is unique. Both boats are of heavy, flat-bottom construction, but the *xavega*, which is 15 to 18 feet long and double-ended with high freeboard, has a most surprising stem form. Figure 6-15 shows this type, and Figure 6-16 shows its structural section. The boat is referred to by the local fishermen as the "Phoenician," but the reason for this name is elusive and speculative. It most obviously must be because

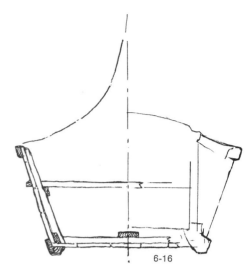

6-15

6-16 *The unique keel-less construction of the flat-bottomed "Phoenician" is shown in this sketch, which represents the cross section amidships. The heavy beaching skids on the outer edges of the bilge perform the double function of providing strength and beaching support. The boats have a bottom curved up at both ends and a transom nearly as broad as the maximum beam amidships.*

6-17 *The typical Peniche lobsterboat is as nicely formed boat of contemporary construction as one can find. These boats, like other Portuguese fishing boats, are measured and recorded officially from a builder's model made after the boat has been built. This boat's waterline aft shows an excessive hollow that mars the overall good lines.*

6-18 *Peniche lobsterboats are commonly beached as shown here because of the lack of well-protected harbors on the exposed Atlantic coast of Portugal. The boats are ruggedly built to withstand this service.*

of the steeply rising bow and stemline, which rises at its extremity in a vertical line to a sharp point, which is some seven to eight feet above the keel. But how are these unschooled fishermen to know that Phoenician boats of 3,000 years ago had vertically rising, extremely high stems?

The other of these two flat-bottomed beach boats, called a *candil,* has the less extreme, more conventional bow of the larger surf boat previously described and has a transom stern.

The remaining type of boat seen at Nazaré is a powerboat of heavy construction. This type is not peculiar to these beaches but is entirely indigenous to Portugal. It is of a style that is much more common in fishing harbors and ports to the south. Since it is heavily built, 22 to 35 feet in length, and fully decked with a heavy diesel engine below, it is not an easy boat to drag out on the beach—but it is often done, sometimes by as many as 20 oxen. These boats are smaller variations of the Peniche-type seiner. They are in truth one step back in the development from the old lateen-rigged double-enders, which were very similar to the boats of the Spanish Mediterranean coast westward of Catalonia. The sterns, while still basically a double ender form, have become broad and rounded. Some still retain the straight outboard sternpost with the rudder hung on it, but the tendency in similar hulls of recent years is toward a rounded, trawler stern. (See Figure 6-17.) These boats are used for lobstering. Typical dimensions are: length, 28 feet; beam, 9.5 feet; and gross tonnage, 4.5.

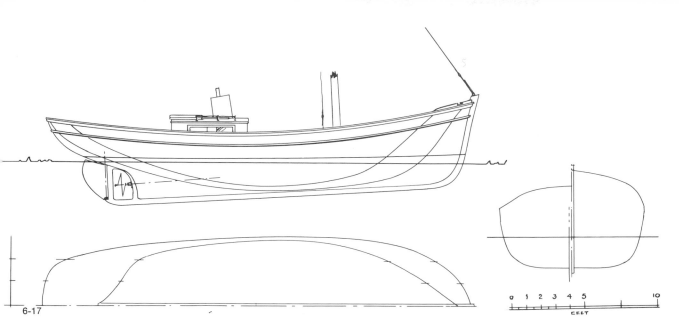

6-17

0 1 2 3 4 5 10

FEET

6-18

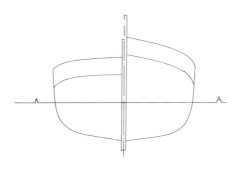
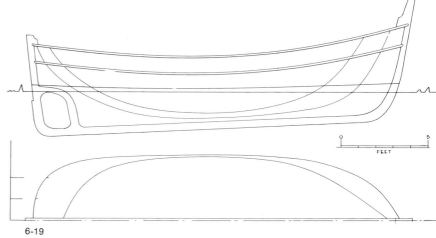

6-19

6-20

6-19   The hull form of the small seiners of the Sesimbra region have much of the same shape and construction as those of the Spanish coast.

6-20   These Sesimbra seiners are hauled out regularly on a ramp. Note the Mediterranean-style stem extension. Boats north of the Tagus River in Portugal do not have this feature.

6-21   The Mediterranean influence of the bow decorations on these boats moored in Sesimbra is typical of the southern, more protected region of Portugal. The elaborate cross and the oculus are common in Iberian boat decor.

6-22   A small fish-landing boat being pulled up on the beach stern first.

6-23   The small fish-landing beach boat used south of the Tagus estuary is a graceful round-bottomed surf-adapted boat. It is light and easily handled by one or two fishermen and has an excellent capacity for its length.

6-21

6-22

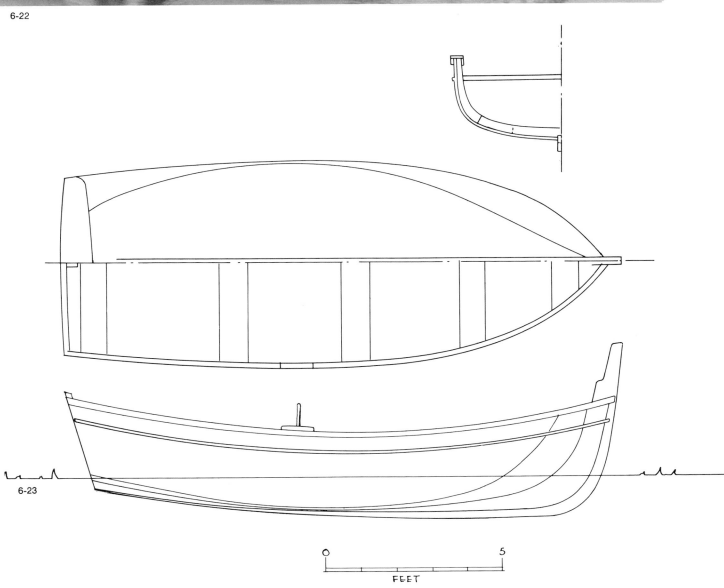

6-23

O   5

FEET

6-24

South of Lisbon a most active boatbuilding and fishing center is located in and about the well-protected harbors and beaches of Sesimbra and Setubal. The boats of this vicinity include the sardine seiners previously discussed and the small lobsterboats above, but the most typical and graceful craft of this coast relate very closely to the lateen-rigged sailing double-enders of recent Mediterranean heritage. Figure 6-19 shows the hull lines of one of these boats typical of many built in Sesimbra. This boat, about 23 feet long and 8 feet in beam, is very similar to the Catalonian beach boats east of Barcelona, which still carry their lateen rig. These boats of Portugal have simply been adapted to power, carrying a small wheelhouse and sometimes a diesel stack. They are always multicolored. Figure 6-20 shows a number of these boats drawn up on the ramp in Sesimbra. Their identity is most immediately revealed by their extended stemposts with caps in the true Mediterranean style. In Figure 6-21 the several boats of this Sesimbra type on moorings show the owners' variable tastes in bow decorations, such as an oculus, a mermaid, and a Portuguese cross.

A very small but charming relative to these "long liners" of Sesimbra is a rather diminutive, one-man pulling boat. In general profile this boat is reminiscent of the candil of Nazaré, but she is a more graceful creature. She is lighter, a little smaller in dimension, round on the bottom, and has a deep transom stern. The hull lines of this boat, shown in Figure 6-23, do not reveal its grace adequately. It is necessary to see one hauled out on the beach or ramp, with its stem pointing toward the sea in the misty light of a waxing sun, to appreciate the rocker keel and arrogant sheer that both blend into the raked stem. They are nice little boats (see Figure 6-22 averaging 14 to 16 feet in length, and are used as fish transporters from the larger boats.

Not all Portuguese fishermen have given up using sail, nor have other workboat sailors, for that matter. On the most southerly coast of Portugal, where the harbors and the people are almost as Spanish as they are Portuguese, there is an exciting tuna industry. Here, sailing out of Faro, Tavira, and other harbors along the Algarve coast, is a style of tuna-fishing boat that is still gracefully propelled by a single, great lateen sail. This boat, again, is very similar to the Mediterranean Catalonian boat, except it has a square, transom stern, rather than being double-ended. Her lines are very similar to those of the Sesimbra boats, combined with the transom of the smaller boat. The rig is purely Spanish lateen with a single, long yard that is even longer than any still used on the Spanish coast. For a boat of 30 feet, the lateen yard is no less than 45 feet long. Figure 6-24 presents the general character of one of these lateen-rigged tuna boats of the Algarve.

As are most of the working boats of continental Europe, the boats of Portugal and southern Spain are slowly changing and adapting to the twentieth century. Power craft are almost universally used,

6-25

nd sails are very rare. Even the old square-sailed
ouro wine boat of the Oporto region is now
nally gone. Where for centuries thousands of
arrels each year of unaged port wine were car-
ied downriver from the vineyards and wineries,
ow they are transported by truck. The Douro
ine boat, which expired in the last years of the
960's, was an ancient, tired, and, certainly, unu-
ual river lighter. Also, and more significantly, it
as in its style and configuration, a traditional riv-
r-to-the-sea boat (see Figure 6-25). The ancient
gyptian boats of the Nile sailed upriver with great
quaresails and long steering sweeps to guide them
hrough the quick turns of the river's bed. The
ine boats of the Douro River in Portugal had
he same long, balanced steering sweeps and tall
quaresails, all used identically, and their hulls
ere the simple form of a slice of melon. Some of
hese hulls may still be seen on the river and in
he estuary at Oporto. They are guided and pro-
elled now in a mastless, humble existence by sev-
ral oarsmen, as lowly cargo lighters in the harbor.

But occasionally too, at Oporto, the cut of the
ld wine boat's squaresail is seen on smaller har-
or craft. The sail is suspended at three points—by
he ends of two sprits at each corner and by the
ast in the middle—with a draped effect. It is
s efficient as a spinnaker on a yacht. Alas, the
ulls are not yacht hulls, but they have lasted
onger. They are worn and paintless but they move
nd work. The body of this very humble small
arbor sailing barge is perhaps the lowest com-
non denominator of Portuguese boatbuilding. It is

*6-24 The tuna-fishing lateener of Tavira is
very much a Mediterranean type of boat. Its
lateen yard is long and its single sail is of the
same cut as that of the Catalonian boats on
the Spanish Mediterranean. The primary
difference in the Portuguese boats is a plumb
mast and a square stern.*

*6-25 A wine boat of Douro and Oporto. The
platform aft is elevated for the helmsman to
see over the stacks of wine casks. Neither the
casks nor the midship mast are shown in this
museum craft.*

so old, worn, tired, and cheaply structured that it seems hardly able to hold itself together another day. Yet it has beneath its crumbling surface a character and charm possessed by nearly all of the Portuguese boats.

None of the small work boats of Portugal are built to architects' drawings. This is not to say that there are not excellent naval architects in Portugal. It is perhaps to say that they are not really needed for the small working craft. The boats are built by skillful hands, guided by experienced eyes and long memories. All boats so built under 25 tons and engaged in the fisheries must conform to government standards of safety and performance. They must all have a stability analysis, requiring cross-curves derived from accurate hull drawings. The builders, therefore, build models of their craft and deliver them to the naval architect of their choice for the required computations. This represents a rare example of marriage between science and native art, and a very useful one. It is a pragmatic means of preservation of whatever valid and confirmed qualities are inherent in the traditional types.

The great old Portuguese flotilla of sailing fishing craft is undergoing a transformation to contemporary technology—one of the last to do so on the European continent. Before World War II, I cruised south from the English Channel and made a landfall in the very early morning on the Portuguese coast. I recall counting more than 100 sails of lateen-rigged sardine boats. As I remember these sails, they were of a variety of weather-stained pastel colors against a distant hazy and fog-banked coastline. It was a thrilling introduction to the great Mediterranean which lay another day away and beyond. Now Portugal is modernizing and rejuvenating its fishing fleet, though I am sure that much traditional construction will prevail.

Iberian culture exists in the Atlantic islands of Madeira, the Canaries, and the Azores. Much of the Madeira-islanders' diet is seafood, and the fish caught here are much the same as those of the near-shore fisheries of Portugal. The boats, however, while operating under oars or with small sails, are obviously much less refined. They are open, with beamy, shallow hulls of most graceful proportions, but they do not have the steeply rising ends so often found on the inshore boats of Portugal. Their most characteristic feature is the nicely rounded profile of the stem post. Beginning at the keel with a gentle continuous arc, the stem projects upward and forward to its simple and undecorated terminal some two feet above the sheer line. The stern post is only slightly lower and similarly curved. The external keel, as well as the stem and stern posts, are notable in the extent of their sided external dimensions beyond the planking at the rabbet. This characteristic feature creates an old and primitive appearance in all these boats. All of the boats are fitted with heavy bilge keels for hauling out on a rugged shingle beach, most of which is heavy cobblestone. There are basically two sizes of these craft; the smaller are approximately 18 feet to perhaps 20 feet in length overall, while the larger are about 35 feet in length. The larger boats are partially decked and today most are motorized. The hull forms of both types are nearly identical, and the predominant choice of color is green with a yellow sheer strake above the rubwale.

The most predominant boat in the Azores, and the only indigenous type, is used for pursuing whales. (See Figure 6-26.) This type was adopted almost without change from the whale boats of more than a century ago. Whaling is a proud and significant industry in the Azores, with the boats operating together in a working federation. The boats are launched from the beach in protected coves and sail after a school of whales under a short sprit or gaff rig. The sails and masts are dropped for the final approach for striking. The entire whale hunt, including the type of boat used, is nearly identical to the much-documented techniques of the nineteenth century New England whaling industry. It is interesting that this part of a great nautical tradition has been preserved in a remote showcase in an insular world. Whaling is a way of life whose future is doubtful, as the whaling industry continues to deteriorate with the depletion of its quarry.

There is perhaps no other region in the western world that has generated a greater variety of indigenous working boats than the Iberian coasts.

This chapter reflects this variety and abundance of both sailing and power craft. There are still some types and variants of types in Portugal that have not been mentioned. The descriptions of the boats of Portugal, while not complete, are, however, perhaps as comprehensive as those in any contemporary survey. The fishing industry in Portugal is, like Norway's, a significant national industry. Unlike Norway's, the techniques of fishing and the types of fish caught are of a great variety, and this difference leads to more numerous types and styles of boats. This, together with the different climate and coastal geography, accounts for greater numbers of smaller craft operating from beaches. The same factors largely account for the existence of the smaller fishing craft in the Mediterranean and the larger more powerful craft in northern Europe.

Portugal is a unique country of contrasts and her boats reflect this. The climate is delightful and sunny, but storm clouds threaten just offshore on the horizon. Portugal has formidable rocky headlands, where enormous Atlantic seas beat continuously. But these same rocky headlands shelter the inviting white sand beaches between. The people, too, are full of contrasts, sad and smiling, proud and humble—their heritage is a strange mixture from the centuries-long Moorish occupation and the struggles of European Christians to regain their lands. The Iberian peninsula, because of its central location, has been the intermediate land between the European north and

6-26 *The Azores whaler is lightly and strongly built. Efficient sailboats, they are operated from the beaches of Fayal.*

6-26

the Mediterranean south. It also leads to the East and to the western hemisphere. On these old and still contemporary trade routes, it is genuinely the crossroads.

With these conflicting mixtures of tradition, which began when the first Phoenician stopped to beach his craft or when some unrecorded earlier civilized sailors visited in search of trade, the Iberian boatbuilders have persisted in their craft. Boatbuilding continues in the traditional manner in such small fishing ports as Sesimbra. The methods and tools of the builders are very old. Building always takes place in the open—sometimes on the beach or beside the road, where the planks and timbers are handcut in open saw pits. Despite these seemingly primitive habits, Iberian boats are exquisitely modeled, and Iberian sailors are as skilled as the best of any country in the basic arts of seamanship. It is only reasonable that this should be so, because these people have been practicing their crafts for about 3,000 years.

American Neptune *(Gillmer)*, 5-21, 5-29, 5-35, 5-36, 5-37, 5-39, 5-43, 5-45, 5-47, 5-50, 5-51; Anchor Light Studio, 2-9; Bald Mountain Boat Works, 3-36; W. H. Ballard *(Cy Cousins)*, 2-10; Bibliotheque and Musée, Marseilles, 1-11, 1-13; Alain Boutry, 3-42, 4-21; Mike Brown, 2-8; John Burgess, 4-14; Roy A. Calvert 2-38, 2-39; Reg. A. Calvert 1-9; City of Hull Museums, 1-5; Costa Naslas, Harry Amanatides, Athens, 1-10, 5-5, 5-6, 5-8; Sidney L. Cullen, 2-14; Robert de Gast, 2-21, 2-25, 2-28, 2-31; Field Museum of Natural History, 1-7; E. E. Fitzgerald, 6-8, 6-13, 6-20, 6-21, 6-22; Ivan Flye, 2-16, 2-18; Greek National Tourist Office, 5-9; Basil Greenhill, 4-15; Oyvind Gulbrantsen, F.A.O., 1-23, 1-24; Handels-og Sofartmuseet *(Henning Henningsen)* Helsingor, Denmark, 3-15, 3-16, 3-17, 3-18, 3-19, 3-24, 3-25, 3-32, 3-33, 3-34; Hudslef *(Ivor Bensen)* Arendel, Norway, 1-17; Italian Government Travel Office, 5-22, 5-23, 5-24; Fenno Jacobs, 5-28; Jenssens Foto, Hougesund, Norway, 4-9; Richard Johns, 2-45, 2-46; Everttt C. Johnson, 2-29; Steven Lang, 4-16; Kevin MacLaverty, 4-29; Galvani de A. Marchi, Cattolica, Italy, 5-17, 5-18, 5-19; James Mavor, 5-33, 6-11, 6-25; John N. Miller & Sons, Ltd., Fife, Scotland, 4-7, 4-8, 4-12, 4-13; National Broadcasting Company, 6-26; National Fisherman, 2-3, 2-17, 2-19, 2-43, 2-49; Nederlandsch Historisch Scheepvaart Museum, Amsterdam, 3-1, 3-2, 3-3, 3-4; Peabody Museum, Salem *(American Neptune)* 5-20, 5-27, 5-38; Richard H. Phillips, 6-5; Royal Scottish Museum, 3-39; The Science Museum, London, 1-18, 1-19, 4-1, 4-2, 4-3, 4-5, 4-11, 4-17, 4-18, 4-20, 4-23, 4-24, 5-1, 5-2, 5-3; David Q. Scott, 2-1, 2-2, 2-4, 2-5, 2-7, 2-27, 3-21, 3-29, 3-38, 5-25, 5-26, 5-44, 6-5, 6-18; Sjöfartsmuseet, Göteborg, S. Notini, Director, 1-16; Skipper Publishing Co., 2-33, 2-35; Skipper Publishing Co. *(R. B. Mitchell)*, 2-42; John Tyrrell, 4-22, 4-25, 4-26, 4-27, 1-15; Universitetets Oldsaksamling, Oslo, 1-1, 1-2, 1-3; Prof. A. S. Yalcin, Istanbul, 5-12, 5-14.